# FOOLS FRIDAY:

An Educator's Journey

# FOOLS FRIDAY:

## An Educator's Journey

by Tom Pike

FONS VITAE

First published in 2022 by
Fons Vitae
49 Mockingbird Valley Drive
Louisville, KY 40207
http://www.fonsvitae.com
Email: fonsvitaeky@aol.com

Library of Congress Control Number: 2022936798
ISBN 978 1 941610 90 9
Printed in USA

For Helen,

    my children Sarah, Catherine, David, and Lisa,

    and their mother Lucy

# CONTENTS

# ACKNOWLEDGEMENTS

*Fools Friday* is comprised of stories of students, teachers, and parents from my forty years working in schools with children and teenagers, twenty-six as founding head of St. Francis High School, a small, independent, progressive high school in Louisville, KY.

My thanks go to the St. Francis students, parents, teachers, and staff, especially for their support of this ongoing experiment in creative, effective, and humane learning.

# AUTHOR'S NOTE

*Fools Friday* is a work of creative nonfiction: the events portrayed actually happened. However, names of students and of most adults have been changed to protect the privacy of those depicted. In addition, identifying details such as genders, ethnicities, familial relationships, and some places of residence may also have been changed. Any unchanged name appears with the explicit consent of the person named.

The creative aspect involves both writing techniques and interpretation of the facts. Art and craft enhance the skeletal facts with the flesh of imagination. For example, when recreating meetings, I provide dialogue which may be word for word from notes I kept or may come from my memory of the meeting as what was probably said. And although I have corroborated details and consulted notes whenever possible, in the end the stories in this book reflect my recollection and record of events.

# 1

## SENIOR PRANK

Roy Harper, head of building maintenance, was waiting for me when I arrived at school at my usual 7:30 am.

"You won't believe it, Tom, but somehow the seniors got in last night even though the security system seems to be working." Not what I wanted to hear. I had been hoping we'd be spared this year.

"What have they done this time?"

"There's no physical damage, but come with me."

Roy, St. Francis High School's Mr. Fix-It, took me into the central courtyard where, forty feet above us, suspended from one of the steel trusses, were a table and a couple of chairs. A banner overhead announced "THE SECURITY SYSTEM SUCKS!" It was signed: "The Seniors." Well, I thought, this is different from previous pranks. As it turned out, it was different only in the kind of damage done. Still, it was hard not to admire the signature SFHS twist on the typical senior prank.

Over the years, members of graduating classes occasionally planned and executed senior pranks. A small group of students would sneak into the school late at night and make a mess: displaced furniture, obscenities on chalkboards, trash tossed everywhere. Physical damage usually occurred: tables with broken legs, graffiti written on walls with permanent markers. Invariably, the perpetrators were identified as they could never resist bragging about their success. They were required to assist the maintenance staff with cleanup and pay for repair or replacement of anything broken.

In May, several weeks before this newest prank, I had met with the senior class to go over end-of-year activities and give my annual let's-be-careful-prom-night-so-that-everyone-graduates talk. I had never before raised the issue of pranks. They didn't happen every year, and I hesitated to put the idea in students' minds just in case it wasn't already there. But, with new facilities and a shared building, I had decided it was worth the risk.

Class advisor Carl Young, Dean of Students Tim Marshall, and I were in the Commons Room with the thirty-six seniors. I chose my words carefully, wanting to say just enough.

"As you know," I started, making eye contact as I looked around the circle of students, "there have been senior pranks in recent years." The word "pranks" immediately got their attention.

"They often caused considerable damage for which the students involved had to pay the school. They disrupted learning and inconvenienced both students and teachers. Last year's prank created a real mess—wet paint on all the chairs. With the apartments in our building we now have close neighbors and overlapping security. There simply can be no more senior pranks and I count on your cooperation."

The students listened and seemed to understand; I saw a few heads nod. I left the meeting hoping that clear expectations and my relationships with individual seniors, together with the new security system and secured key setup, would be sufficient deterrent.

Two weeks later, throughout the morning after the prank, the scope of its impact quickly grew. Teachers reported that rooms had been unlocked, desks opened, personal computers accessed, and furniture rearranged. Tim's office had been filled floor-to-ceiling with wadded up newspapers. I was relieved to learn that other administrative offices had been spared. I both admired and cursed their ingenious scheme. The creative and independent thinking, painstaking planning, and resourceful execution were exactly the skills St. Francis aims to cultivate in their students. And in one way, they had obeyed my prohibition—the prank was completely non-destructive in terms of physical stuff. But they had broken it in other ways. Learning the appropriate and responsible use of their skills is especially difficult for teenagers.

When I saw Roy later, he was frowning. "Tom, I have no idea how, but the security cameras were shut down for several hours and then turned back on, leaving the digital records of the thirty cameras blank for that period."

By end of day, nine seniors were identified as the perpetrators, five boys and four girls—a fourth of the class. Led by three computer wizards, Dan, Will, Leon, and climbing expert Jack, the group, pleased with itself, proudly boasted of their success in pulling off a harmless, overnight prank. I learned that they had started planning the prank when they were in the ninth grade. They told me that they had been inspired by the memory of Fools Fridays when Leon was a younger student at St. Francis School in Goshen. As he put it, "We thought that a good prank would provide a change of pace from the daily routine of classes." And I thought to myself that Frank Cayce, were he still alive, would be pleased and amused at this legacy of his years as Head at St. Francis School.

Everything had been ready to go weeks before I made my speech and the group's momentum was such that what I said had no impact on them. The only risk they had considered was the possibility of someone getting injured, which they felt highly unlikely. They also persuaded themselves that they were helping the school by exposing the vulnerability of the security system. I marveled, yet again, at the ingenuity and the shortsightedness of the adolescent mind. When confronted, they seemed genuinely surprised at how upset we were.

Starting with Dan, I interviewed each of them. He was one of the brightest students at St. Francis as well as a talented actor, and a determined but average long-distance runner. Dan was ever ingenious and, like many adolescents, also ingenuous—open, frank, and candid. While not exactly cocky, he assumed he could accomplish anything he wanted. He was always involved in too many projects, both in and out of school. He had been in my office a number of times, not for being in trouble, but as my computer troubleshooter. A fellow Apple fan, Dan could sit down at my iBook and, his nimble fingers dancing across the keyboard, quickly fix whatever problem I had. I was fond of Dan; he was one of the seniors I knew best.

"We need to talk about what happened, Dan. Have a seat."

Laid back as usual, he plopped down in a chair. "Sure, what do you want to know?"

"Tell me first how you got in the building?"

"It was easy. We knew Ms. Marcum had a master key in her receptionist's desk. We took it one afternoon after she went home, had it copied, and slipped it back in her desk before she arrived the next morning."

Dan's face was relaxed, his voice calm as he patiently answered my questions, not nervous, not smug, just proud. No guilt, no remorse. A damage-free prank.

"But I thought those keys couldn't be copied."

"We learned that months ago when we first tried to get copies made. So Leon searched the Internet, located a source of blanks, and bought three boxes. We knew a regular locksmith wouldn't make copies, but figured a big store would be less careful. I went to three different locations and each one made a box of copies for me."

"What about the security system. How on earth did you disable and reactivate it?"

"That was Leon's main job. He located the system's operating manual online and downloaded a copy. Since the system was connected to the school's wireless network, he was able to access it from the garage next door with his laptop. You guys made it easy by leaving the default passwords in the system's computers."

"Did you ever think about the risks of shutting down the school's security?"

"Nothing was damaged, Mr. Pike. The system is working fine."

"That's not what I'm talking about, Dan," my voice edged with impatience. "But I'll meet with all of you together once I finish interviewing the other students." Dan looked puzzled as he left. Good, I thought, maybe he'll think some more about what he did.

Helen came in next, tearful and distraught. An average student and dedicated volleyball player, she had many friends, cared about everyone. I knew that Tim Marshall had already reprimanded her for unlocking and messing up his office. I got up from my chair, asked her to close the door, and gestured for her to sit in the chair next to mine.

"Helen, what all of you did may have seemed a lark at the time, but was truly serious. "

"Mr. Pike, I'm really sorry," she began, her voice trembling. "I'm concerned about Marshall. He's helped me so much and I just hate seeing him angry. I wouldn't have made it through St. Francis without him. I never expected him to be so upset. All we did was fill his office with wads of paper and then leave a funny message on his computer. We thought he would see it as a big joke."

I thanked Helen for her apology, told her that I planned to meet with all the seniors later that day, and let her go. I could tell that she had already absorbed what I needed her to know. Too often adults think teenagers need a tirade or a sermon, when a few words and appropriate consequences are more effective.

By the end of the day, I finished talking individually with the students involved. Several had apologized, but most of them seemed clueless as to the seriousness of their actions. Tim and I met that afternoon with all thirty-six seniors in Carl's classroom on the third floor, where I spoke to the pranksters in the presence of their classmates. The nine sat in front so I could look directly at them as I talked.

"Some of you are puzzled at the staff's response since you went to such pains not to destroy anything. But caught up with the cleverness of your prank, you overlooked several important issues.

"You disabled for a considerable period the school's security system and placed at jeopardy not only the school's security but the security of the entire building. You stole a master key from a staff member's desk and made copies of it. You went into locked classrooms and offices and messed with personal property of teachers by opening their desks and accessing their computers. These actions were violations of the basic trust and mutual respect at the heart of this school and far more destructive than any physical damage."

I paused for a minute. The room was quiet. The expressions on the faces of the nine offenders ranged from impatience and puzzlement to attentiveness.

"When I met with all of you last week, I explained that there could be no more senior pranks and asked for your cooperation. I outlined the problems, especially in a shared building. Some of you ignored my request and proceeded with your plans. Mr. Marshall and I will decide on what punishment you deserve and let you know tomorrow."

The consequences for the nine students included personal apologies to the staff, working for the school on two days when other seniors were excused, and sharing payment of the $1,000 cost of re-keying the one hundred and eight locks of the building.

When two weeks earlier I had asked for the seniors' cooperation, I knew I was taking a risk, putting my relationships with them on the line. Educators in small schools bear an authority and vulnerability similar to parents with their children. Students feel personally known by us, yet we are the adults, mentors of their development, responsible for setting expectations and enforcing accountability. When unexpected, undesirable behaviors inevitably occur, perspective and equanimity are critical. We feel and express disappointment and follow with reasonable consequences, a response more likely to change behavior than if we respond from anger. But Dean Tim Marshall and advisor Carl Young were furious that the students had ignored my request for cooperation. Tim posted a letter to the seniors telling them he would not be attending their senior luncheon. Carl, who had been selected by the seniors to speak at graduation, informed them that he would not be speaking, punishing the entire class, not just the perpetrators.

The prank, which was in fact brilliantly planned and executed, did provide helpful, important information about the security of the school. Leon and Dan showed Roy Harper how they had located the website where they found the instruction manual for the security system and suggested appropriate passwords. They also gave him the online source for the supposedly secure key blanks.

While still surprised by the staff's response, the perpetrators cheerfully completed their punishment and, at the end of May, it was my pleasure to preside over their graduation. But there was one further dilemma. The student I had chosen for the Head of School's award was a leader of the pranksters. Do I skip giving an award this year? Do I give it to someone not as well suited for the award, but who hadn't taken part? If I give the award to my original choice in the face of his lapse of judgment, what message does that convey?

I decided to stay with Dan, my original choice. I believed that he would learn more from a decision expressing my faith in his potential than from an additional punishment for a lapse of judgment.

I retired from the school in 2003. When I saw Tim a couple of years later, I asked him if there had been any recent senior pranks. "No, and it's really interesting. Evidently, none of the seniors in the last couple of classes have been able to think of a way to top the brilliant success of this Class. It's like the bar had been set so high, no one wants to risk a lesser prank." He hoped it was over, but given the nature of adolescence, he and I both knew that sooner or later we would again be surprised. Sometimes the surprises were heartbreaking, always they were fraught with challenges for both adults and adolescents. They always combined for me the carnival spirit of Fools Friday and the essential Quaker belief that each of us has the divine, the sacred within us. In teenagers both qualities are close to the surface and can burst forth at any moment. My job was to find a way to let this happen while initiating our students into a world that mostly forbade both. It didn't always work. But, like our students, I learned as much from the failures as from the successes.

# 2

## F.O.I.L.

Mike, Dale, Steve, and Chris were the regulars at the weekly meetings of the St. Stephen's School Auto Club. Cars and auto mechanics were virtually the only interest the four boys had in common. Mike was from Mexico City, tall, urbane and artistic. He and I had designed and built sets for recent Drama Club productions of Melville's *Billy Budd* and Shaw's *Heartbreak House*. Dale, one of my pre-calculus students, loved problem solving. Shy, immature, his agile mind never seemed to stop whirring. Steve, one of my advisees, was from Pittsburgh. Preppy and earnest, not academically inclined, he struggled with most of his classes, but at fourteen had all the people skills he would later use to become a successful businessman. Chris was a solid student, sociable and easygoing, one of those kids you never worry about.

The Auto Club met on Sunday afternoons, a welcome change from the week's classes. The four regulars and I turned part of an unused dairy barn on the school's farm into a shop, bought a set of tools, and went to work. For the first project, we stripped a 1954 FireDome DeSoto sedan down to the bare chassis and rebuilt its classic "hemi" V-8 engine. We had brought the non-running engine to the school in the back of a farm truck. We put the engine back in the chassis, installed a bench seat for a driver and two passengers, and rigged a rudimentary instrument panel. Not roadworthy, but we could drive the resurrected skeleton car around the farm property. As we had only a couple of hours for the weekly work sessions, it took five months to complete the job.

The day finally came to start the rebuilt engine. We poured gasoline into the fuel tank, checked the oil, opened the barn door wide open, and gathered around the greasy, barebones vehicle. I had announced the big event at lunch and a number of students came out to the barn to see what we had been doing all this time.

"Okay, guys. It's the moment of truth," I proclaimed. "Pick a number between one and twenty to decide who will start the engine. Mike?" "Nine." "Cliff?" "Sixteen." "Dale?" "Eleven." "Steve?" "Six." Dale, astutely reading his math teacher's mind, won the honor by choosing eleven, a prime number in the middle.

With a big smile on his face, Dale climbed up into the driver's seat, put his foot on the accelerator, his hand on the key, and focused his eyes on the engine four feet in front of him. As we held our collective breaths, Dale slowly turned the key, engaging the starter. The reborn engine came to life immediately, erupting with an ear-splitting, BA-ROOM blast of sound—we had installed hot rod headers with no mufflers. Then the engine settled down to a steady, roaring, burbling beat as eight big cylinders, fed by a four-barrel carburetor, fired in rapid order. We whooped and hollered over the din, grinning and laughing, slapping each other on the back, excited at successfully completing a long, hard, challenging job.

I spent four years in the early 1960s at what I will here call St. Stephen's, a small boarding school for boys, which I found to be traditional and rule-bound, with strong academic, athletic, and service programs, and required chapel. The setting was idyllic, a cluster of stone buildings overlooking a lake, surrounded by woods and fields.

I started the St. Stephen's Auto Club as a way of getting to know some of the teenage students better. At that time, Lucy and I had three children: one, four, and five years old. Being the father of young children at the same time I was teaching adolescents, human development intrigued me. I was curious about the influences which formed the individual personalities and intellects of my students.

I realized that extra-curricular activities providing out-of-class opportunities for teachers and students to work together are essential to a good high school. In their struggle with emerging adult identities, adolescents need friends and mentors who are not their parents.

At St. Stephen's, the Auto Club was the obvious choice as I had worked on cars since I was sixteen and knew that some of the students shared my interest. Such experiences—firing up a newly rebuilt engine, the smooth performance of a play after weeks of rehearsals, an athletic team hitting its stride in the season's last game and upsetting an arch-rival—are often what adults remember most from their high school years. Unfortunately, those memories rarely include an academic accomplishment. I began to think how classroom learning might become as engaging and satisfying as rebuilding a car, being in a play, or playing on a tcam.

Like most new teachers, I was naive and full of idealism. I had spent many of my years as a student being bored and was impatient with traditional approaches. St. Stephen's math department was experimenting with textbooks which employed "new math." Students first learned why a particular algorithm (a set of rules for solving a problem) worked, and then how to apply it. If students understood the "whyness" of the rules, they would be much more likely to remember them; at least, that was the theory. I had loved math in school and this approach appealed to me. But some of my students were weak in math and struggled to understand abstract concepts. In reality, the textbook authors and I were wearing blinders. The "new math" texts turned out to have been written by mathematicians for mathematically inclined students.

It was Johnny, a ninth grader in my algebra class, who opened my eyes to this fact. Small in size, he had a natural athlete's beautifully proportioned physique. Quick and agile, he excelled in football and wrestling but struggled as a student, especially in math. He was failing algebra until a math department colleague, Howard Schmolze, stepped in as tutor. Howard, a veteran of three decades of teaching, was known for his ability to work with less able students.

One day in class, I was teaching how to multiply two binomials, like $(x + 2)$ times $(x + 7)$. I demonstrated without naming it how the algorithm called F.O.I.L. could be derived using an elegant four-step proof, I wrote out the proof on the blackboard, going carefully from step to step. This way, when I introduced the F.O.I.L. rule in the next day's class, I expected the students not just to have memorized the rule, but to understand why it worked. I finished the proof with a flourish and turned around to discover blank expressions on the faces of Johnny and most of the rest of the class. Ignoring the obvious message, I dutifully followed the teacher's manual and put the students to work multiplying some binomials, using the long, four-step derivation to reinforce why the shortcut worked.

Johnny raised his hand and I went over to his desk. "Mr. Pike, I'm confused. Can you help me? Mr. Schmolze showed me a much easier way to do this. It's called F.O.I.L., which stands for first, outside, inside and last. Can I show you?"

"Sure, Johnny," I said, pleased with his interest, as he rarely volunteered anything in class. He continued with unexpected confidence. "All you have to do is multiply together the first parts of each binomial and then the outside parts, the inside parts, and finally the last parts, then add like terms and you've got it. I'll do one for you," he said, excitedly. He wrote down a problem from the assignment I had just given them, $(x + 3) (x + 8)$, and began, "To F.O.I.L. it, I take x times x, that's F for first, then x times 8, that's O for outside, then 3 times x, that's I for inside, and then 3 times 8, L for last, and add them all together, combining like terms."

He had written: $(x+3)(x+8) = x^2 + 8x + 3x + 24 = x^2 + 11x + 24$

"See how much easier that is," he said, pleased with himself.

"It certainly is," I humbly replied, two thoughts bouncing in my head: *So much for new math* and *This may be the first time Johnny's ever been excited in a math class.* "Tomorrow I want you to show the rest of the class your and Mr. Schmolze's shortcut."

Thanks to Johnny, I learned to make math as simple as possible. I did, however, continue to use proofs and derivations of algorithms for extra credit problems for the handful of gifted students who enjoyed such challenges.

I soon discovered several colleagues who shared my frustration with what we saw as the school's lack of creativity and focus on control. We were always complaining about the tedious, biweekly faculty meetings, which typically lasted at least two hours and were spent mostly discussing school rules and how to enforce them. I remember one meeting when the Assistant Headmaster took what seemed like an hour to harangue us about enforcing the hair rule. (A student's hair could not touch his shirt collar.) In his clipped, New England voice he instructed us to closely examine the back of students' necks to see if any hairs touched the collar of their shirts. "Make sure their ties are pulled snug. If any hairs touch, write them up for a two demerit penalty." Sam, Louie, Mike and I looked at each other and rolled our eyes.

We four malcontents were all around thirty. Sam was a tall, lanky, laconic math teacher from Bardstown, Kentucky. Casual in manner

23

and dress, Sam was a cynic. Mike, who taught Greek and Latin, was a brilliant British classicist from Oxford University. Thick glasses, tie loosened, and shirttails half-out, he was a gifted linguist, superb debater, and perhaps the brightest of all the teachers. Louie from Alabama, pudgy, with thinning hair, loved literature, kids, and social activism.

Louie's students loved and admired him in return. The 1989 film, *Dead Poets Society*, starring Robin Williams, was set in 1959 at Welton Academy, a fictitious boys boarding school. It was actually filmed at St. Stephen's School. Williams portrayed an impulsive, irrepressible English teacher who would go to any extreme to wake up his students to great literature. His character reminded me of a slightly over-the-top version of Louie Crew. Like most gifted teachers I have known, Louie was passionate about his subject and had energy, creativity, and an original teaching style. A decade later, these were the qualities I would seek when hiring teachers for St. Francis High School.

There were many stories about Louie's antics in the classroom, but my favorite was the day he sent a message to his students that he wasn't feeling well. He left instructions for them to come up to his apartment. They arrived to find him wearing a gold satin dressing gown over his clothes, ensconced in his canopied, four-poster bed. He served them tea and madeleines, while they discussed Proust's *Swann's Way*, the novel they were currently reading.

I enjoyed teaching, but became restless and began looking for additional challenges. I took on a variety of administrative jobs—admissions, financial aid, college advising, and scheduling. Applying my problem-solving skills to a school enterprise rather than to a business was exciting and satisfying. I loved the multi-layered puzzle of creating a class schedule that fit requests of both students and teachers into available rooms and time slots. Using linear programming skills I had learned at Stanford, I devised an admissions formula to predict an applicant's success at St. Stephen's. Today, computers can do this in seconds. Back in 1966, I went to the school's business office and spent many afternoons using big, clunky Freiden mechanical calculators with the whirring, clattering musical sound of many gears turning incessantly. The quiet of today's computers still seems eerie and mysterious to me.

Concurrently with expanding the scope of my job, I became actively involved with my children's education. Sarah was five, and Lucy and I found a nearby cooperative kindergarten being organized by a group of parents interested in a progressive, developmental approach. Cathy followed Sarah at the kindergarten and Sarah enrolled in the first grade at the local public elementary school, which was the only option available to us. As a traditional school with a lockstep approach—everyone did the same things at the same time, different readiness levels be damned—it was a disaster for Sarah. She simply wasn't comfortable reading aloud sentences like "See Jill run." I remember having to carry her, crying, up the steps of the school bus. I became involved with some of the kindergarten parents and several St. Stephen's faculty members to start an independent, developmentally based elementary school in a nearby town that would survive into the next century. Sarah thrived after entering the second grade and Cathy soon joined her there.

As I look back at my four years at St. Stephen's, I realize how much I absorbed that influenced my evolving educational philosophy. I learned that students are always watching, listening, and absorbing. The St. Stephen's teenagers got a clear message about priorities when they saw faculty members spend more time and energy enforcing the hair, tie, and tucked-in-shirt rules than finding creative ways to teach their courses. I decided that a school rule is viable and necessary only if it enhances learning or increases mutual respect. I am unaware of any credible research which shows that students in schools with dress codes and uniforms learn more than students in schools without dress restrictions. Unless a student's appearance is distracting to learning or disrespectful to others, it shouldn't be an issue. Wanting to experiment with appearance, with one's identity, is a natural part of adolescence.

In my twenty-six years at St. Francis High School, I remember just a couple of times when I had to ask students to change their clothes. One day, Adam, a mischievous tenth grader, came to school wearing a long skirt. I knew him well enough to be confident that his cross-dressing was purely an attention-getting stunt. His appearance was disruptive to learning because of the distraction it created in his classes without raising any issues for discussion in return. I took him aside between classes, informed him that his appearance was disruptive, and told him to change clothes, which he did without argument. When a provocative ninth grade girl arrived at school in a skirt so short and top so scant that her presence was distracting to classmates and teachers, her female English teacher successfully addressed the situation with a frank, but sensitive conversation.

At St. Stephen's, I discovered and claimed my calling as an educator both in the classroom and in the dairy barn on Sundays with the Auto Club. The kind of education I desired could never happen at a traditional school. I decided to look for a new job, one that was primarily administrative, yet involving teaching and other contact with students, girls and boys. I chose to stay in independent schools, which are typically smaller than public schools and give leaders greater autonomy and flexibility to set school policy and hire personnel. Charter schools didn't exist yet and public schools would not have hired me; lacking an education degree and certification, I would have been considered unqualified for either teaching or administrative positions.

Frank Cayce, the father of Gordon, one of my St. Stephen's math students, had been hired a year earlier to head St. Francis School, a new, innovative, preschool through eighth grade independent school

26

in my hometown of Louisville, Kentucky. Gordon told his father about my desire to leave St. Stephen's. In February 1967, Frank and I met over drinks and dinner at a conference in Washington, D.C. Frank was in his fifties and had been an Episcopal priest for a decade. Being Headmaster of St. Francis School was his first school job. It was most unusual for someone with no training or experience to be hired to head a school and I wasn't sure what to expect.

We found each other in the ornate, luxurious lobby of the Shoreham Hotel alongside Rock Creek Park. Frank was outgoing and welcoming, heavyset, well-dressed in a tailored suit, striped shirt, and colorful tie. We each had a bourbon in our hands before finding a table and quickly discovered a compatibility of ideas about kids and learning. While he had never taught, Frank had been involved for several years with a school for kids with learning problems when he was rector of a small parish in Virginia. He became fascinated with developmental education, matching the needs of individual students with activities appropriate for their readiness levels. This was the approach that had benefited my oldest daughter Sarah, and, to me, made sense for all students. I was intrigued with the prospect of applying progressive ideas to older students. While Frank was interested in me because of my experiences with adolescents, he also knew my administrative experience would be a great help to him in developing St. Francis School. He proposed to me the job of Assistant Headmaster, coupled with teaching a math class. I accepted his offer and looked forward to working with Frank at St. Francis School, and to more students like Johnny who would explain to me how F.O.I.L. worked.

# 3

## FOOLS FRIDAY

"Tom, it's time for Fools Friday!"

Frank had called me into his office on a sunny day in April. It was mid-afternoon and he was resting his ample body on the large couch not far from his desk. Frank's tie was loosened and his tweed sports coat lay across a nearby chair. I had no idea what Fools Friday was, but, having worked for eight months with headmaster Frank Q. Cayce, I knew that anything was possible at St. Francis School.

Frank sat up and continued, "I get the feeling that everyone needs a break at least once a year from the daily routine. So, in secret, we plan a special day for the whole school."

"You don't warn the teachers?" I was incredulous, but curious.

With childlike excitement in his voice, "Oh no, Tom, it needs to be a surprise. Not knowing ahead of time is part of the fun. Next Friday, we'll let school start, just like any other day. Teachers will begin the day's activities—reading groups, math, whatever they have planned. After about half an hour, we'll spring Fools Friday."

He pointed to the wall behind me at a large, colorful, paper-mâché mask depicting a joyful sun's face, one of many vibrant student-made artworks in his office.

"That's my Fools Friday mask," he chortled gleefully.

Driving home that night, I was amused by my ambivalent feelings about Fools Friday. During the previous four years I had spent at St. Stephen's School, I became impatient with the tight rule-bound control, which stifled creativity, but I had learned the need for clear expectations and appropriate, consistent consequences. Working with Frank taught me the value of spontaneity in motivating students. He believed that, in the right school setting, every student would be motivated to eventually learn what each of them needed. Though truly appealing to me, it still seemed unrealistic.

Over the next couple of days Frank and I met several times and planned a full day of field trips, a picnic lunch, games, and a couple of short films. Fools Friday was meant to be a change of pace and a time for everyone to become better acquainted: many of the activities brought together students of different ages and grade levels.

Friday morning, Frank put on the large orange and yellow sun mask and moved quickly from classroom to classroom, pulling open the doors, leaping in, shouting "Fools Friday." Students who were old hands at Fools Friday cheered wildly as new students looked bewildered. Teachers' faces took on a variety of expressions, depending on their tolerance for surprise and shelving a day's lesson plans.

Fools Friday turned out to be a productive day. A cross between Santa Claus and Peter Pan, Frank thrived as master of ceremonies and head cheerleader. I was stage manager, shifting students from group to group and moving groups from activity to activity. The few grumbling teachers, who initially bemoaned the loss of a teaching day, ended up with smiles on their faces. We did receive a few calls from parents wondering what their tuition dollars had purchased. We reminded them that they had chosen the school for its innovative approaches to learning. While obviously a day of play, Fools Friday had useful purposes: acquiring and using new skills with collaborative interaction among older and younger students. As Frank knew well, learning and play were not mutually exclusive.

Frank had been hired in 1965 to develop the new independent elementary school that had just been started by St. Francis in the Fields Episcopal Church. Founded as an alternative to Louisville's existing public and private schools, St. Francis School was to be progressive and student-centered. Frank Cayce was an unlikely choice to develop a new school. He had attended LSU and Emory, but had never earned an undergraduate degree. As his wife, Madeline, explained to me, "Frank just enjoyed being a student. He was at Emory, midway through his fifth year, when his father called and told him to come home and get to work. He realized that Frank was never going to graduate and was tired of supporting him." Frank returned home to Hopkinsville, Kentucky, and, after spending a couple of years in the Navy, ran a men's clothing store. He became active in the local Episcopal Church and in Diocesan activities. In 1952, at the encouragement of the Bishop of Kentucky, who needed new clergy for the Diocese, Frank went to Virginia Episcopal Seminary, graduated, and was ordained a priest in 1954.

"Madeline," I asked once, "how was Frank accepted by Virginia Seminary when he hadn't graduated from college?" She laughed, "Oh, Tom, you knew Frank. He called the admissions people after being turned down and somehow convinced them he should come to Alexandria for an interview, even though they said they didn't do interviews. Once he met with them in person, he convinced them to accept him. He always was a great salesman." Frank was serving as pastor of a small church in Virginia, when Steve Davenport, the rector of St. Francis in the Fields Church, hired him to come and direct St. Francis School.

Frank Cayce turned out to be just what the new school needed for a leader and what I needed as a mentor. While confident of my intellectual abilities, I was shy, reserved, and socially inept. Frank was socially at ease anywhere, with anyone. His lack of experience was actually beneficial, as he had no preconceptions about what a school should be. I approached tasks analytically. He was intuitive, a gifted "primitive" educator, with remarkable instincts about different ways to engage students in active learning. Frank understood a child's natural curiosity and innate energy for learning new things.

In the October 1992 St. Francis School newsletter, *The Abacus*, a former student recalled an unforgettable conversation he had had with Frank during his sixth-grade year.

> My father decided he wanted to take me on my first skiing trip out west. Being somewhat of a compulsive child, I worried about the classes and homework I would miss and how I would make it up. My concerns found their way to Mr. Cayce and he called me into his office .... He sat me down and told me he heard I was planning to miss a week of school on the ski slopes. I was preparing to apologize and explain that my father gave me no choice. I hoped he would explain to my father how harmful this vacation would be to my future ... Mr. Cayce had no such intentions. He told me he thought it was a wonderful idea and I shouldn't worry about school at all. He said that learning comes from many places, not just four walls in a class. ... I was slightly confused, because Headmasters were not supposed to say such things, but I was also relieved. (p. 4)

Frank and I became a congenial and effective team. I had sufficient experience to take care of the administrative details of running a school. He used his salesmanship and charm to sell a progressive educational philosophy to a conservative community. Intellectually curious, Frank was a voracious reader, and we shared eclectic interests in films and books. He had a keen sense of color and a flair for graphic design. The walls of the hallways and classrooms were vibrantly painted—red, blue, yellow, green, orange, and purple. Posters, fabric wall hangings, paintings and drawings by both students and professional artists were everywhere. Visitors to St. Francis School knew immediately that they were in a different kind of school.

Visual literacy was an integral part of the school's curriculum. Students at all levels learned to draw, paint, and work with clay and other three-dimensional media. The most unusual component of arts education was the regular viewing of films, thanks to Frank's encyclopedic knowledge of the genre. We watched Charlie Chaplin, Laurel and Hardy, Marcel Marceau, and Robert Flaherty's classic documentaries *Nanook of the North* and *Men of Aran*. We regularly watched imaginative short films, the best source being the National Film Board of Canada. Not all the films shown were avant-garde: a particularly popular choice with students was the 1936 serial, *Flash Gordon.*

Searching for more effective ways to teach children, Frank and I joined the wave of school reform that was part of the societal upheaval in America during the late 1960s and early 1970s. The main influences on our evolving educational philosophy were progressive education, Montessori schools, the British Integrated Day program, and open education. We read articles and books by authors such as John Holt, Jean Piaget, Robert Coles, and A. S. Neill. We visited other schools to see innovative programs in action. We were in the early stages of planning new facilities and keenly interested in how the physical design of schools could facilitate new approaches to learning we wanted to adopt, such as multiage grouping and team teaching.

While most popular during the early and mid-twentieth century, the progressive movement continues to influence educators. Curricula and classroom practice are oriented toward individual student needs and interests and oppose formalized authoritarian procedures. John Dewey (1859-1952), philosopher and educator, was the leader of this movement. Through his writing, teaching, and founding the Laboratory School at the University of Chicago, Dewey has long been associated with the advocacy of schools that are child-centered and emphasize learning through doing.

Proponents of standardized testing and "lockstep" curricula have always dismissed this approach as experimental and permissive. But rigor and discipline can be present or absent in either a traditional or progressive setting. The greatest challenge for a progressive school is to ensure that each student eventually acquires essential skills, yet according to their own developmental clock.

Teacher and writer John Holt's first two books, *How Children Fail* (1964) and *How Children Learn* (1967), were major influences in the open education reform movement that began in the mid-sixties. They became our primers. Holt's straightforward approach made sense to us. In *How Children Learn*, he says:

> We do things backwards. We think in terms of getting a skill first, and then finding useful and interesting things to do with it. The sensible way, the best way, is to start with something worth doing, and then, moved by the strong desire to do it, get whatever skills are needed. If we begin by helping children feel that reading and writing are ways of talking to and reaching other people, we will not have to bribe and bully them into acquiring the skills; they will want them for what they can do with them. (p. 112)

Frank and I were alike in being self-taught educators, open to any structure or curriculum which we believed would enhance learning. We bounced ideas back and forth continually, almost always agreeing on what we should implement. But in ways small and large, we differed dramatically. In my thirties, with young children and a wife in medical school, I stayed close to home by inclination and necessity, getting back and forth to school with four kids in our VW bus. Frank was twenty years older, his children grown, and he drove a Buick convertible. A true bon vivant, he loved social gatherings and conversation. Frank knew people everywhere—filmmakers in California, editors in New York City, landed gentry in Virginia. Frank enjoyed fine clothes, good food, strong drink, and lively company. When taking trips to see schools and attend conferences, he connected with friends and preferred expensive hotels. Frank's fun-loving penchant for extravagance created an underlying tension between the two of us and with the school's Board of Directors. The budget rarely was balanced during those early years.

I remember a trip in 1968, when Frank and I went to New York City to visit two well-known innovative schools, Dalton in Manhattan, and Whitby in nearby Greenwich, Connecticut. One night we had dinner with egghead T. George Harris, a bureau chief with *Time Magazine* and founding editor of *Psychology Today*. I mostly listened as Frank and George argued about whether humanistic education could prevent sociopathic behavior and Rogerian psychology could cure depression. The next night we went for drinks and dinner at the Rainbow Room at Rockefeller Center. We stayed at the Carlyle Hotel, where, drinking late another night, we listened to jazz legend Bobby Short.

During the day we went shopping and visited Dalton and Whitby. Both visits had a heady and visceral impact on us. While we had read about such schools, neither of us had actually visited an open or progressive school, much less two of the best in the country. In front of our eyes was living proof that students could work independently or in small groups, with adults serving primarily as resources and guides to help students accomplish learning projects in a variety of traditional subject areas. At both schools we were surprised when no one paid any attention to visitors walking by or even stopping to observe an activity. Students were reading, calculating, constructing, assembling, experimenting, moving about, and talking—engaged in learning—in an active, busy, buzzing, but in no way permissive environment.

Located on Manhattan's Upper East Side, Dalton School was founded in 1919 by the progressive educator Helen Parkhurst. Inspired by John Dewey, she created the Dalton Plan, which uses learning contracts to promote independent learning. Students' programs were tailored to their individual needs, interests, and abilities. After wandering unaccompanied through the school for several hours observing and talking with students and teachers, we met with Donald Barr, the witty and provocative headmaster. Barr was a well-known critic of the "mind-strangling" orthodoxy of the educational establishment as well as a foe of permissiveness, in school or at home.

Donald Barr and Frank Cayce were both tall, portly, nattily dressed, loquacious extroverts. Both were sophisticated, but one was a lifelong New Yorker, the other a refugee from Western Kentucky. Barr was a consummate achiever with impressive credentials—a student of mathematics and anthropology as an undergraduate at Columbia, teacher of English for ten years at Columbia, author of books on mathematics for children, and a regular contributor of book reviews to *Saturday Review* and *The New York Times*. Barr's critique of education, *Who Pushed Humpty Dumpty?*, is as provocative and relevant today as when it was published in 1971.

I remember standing in a hallway listening to the two of them talk. I was enjoying their verbal repartee when Barr addressed a concern which I had. "Mr. Cayce," he said, "we have many visitors who are impressed with the self-directed learning they see at Dalton. But they miss the underlying, highly organized structure of expectations and accountability which the contracts provide. They don't realize that teachers and administrators must be more skilled and work harder in progressive schools. Simply turning students loose to pursue individual interests can easily become indulgence, not education." I thought to myself, he's right, and it's going to depend on me to create and oversee the necessary structure at St. Francis.

While the majority of Montessori schools are preschools, some have primary grades, and a few extend the approach into higher grades. Whitby, one of the best-known Montessori schools in America, has students from toddlers to teenagers. Montessori is an experiential approach, which combines highly structured activities with individual learners choosing both activity and pace.

We talked at length with Jack Blessington, Whitby's Headmaster. He and Frank had been friends ever since they were together at a summer workshop for new headmasters. Jack was a character— irreverent, funny, deeply serious about his work—a mix of Frank and me. He was closer to my age than Frank's and was simultaneously casual and intense, his youthful face framed by a bushy beard and an unruly thatch of hair. Like me, he had young children who attended his school, one of the reasons he had become an educator. Like Frank, he came from a business background. Jack believed that the Montessori method and the British Integrated Day program had important similarities and that both were exemplary of open education. In his 1974 book, *Let My Children Work!*, Jack describes open schools:

> To "open" a program is to permit the learner to seek with mind
> and hands and feet and ears and nose. To "open" education is
> to reduce immobility and invite movement and exploration.
> It emphasizes process rather than correct answers. This

36

approach suggests that if you seek, you will find; if you knock, a door will open and you will discover an idea or at least feel the joy of finding something. If a teacher supplies everything, however, you stretch out your hand only and not your mind. If a school restricts your use of space, you close out exploration. If you keep hearing "no," you soon stop asking. Open education calls for a total mobilization of the school as a locus—a place—of learning activity. (p. 63)

Whitby truly was a place of active learning. Everywhere we looked, children were involved with colorful, hands-on materials— blocks, puzzles, books, Cuisenaire Rods. Montessori materials are sequentially ordered by design to take a child, working independently, through activities of increasing expectation and complexity. Teachers moved back and forth among their students, responding to a raised hand, praising a child for completion, and making sure each had what they needed to progress. I was amazed at the purposeful, productive atmosphere, with students working comfortably at individually appropriate levels. They were neither being held back by immature or less able students nor being rushed or shamed by students moving more quickly. While I concluded that the time spent working independently should be balanced with small group collaborative learning, Whitby was the best example I had seen of the developmental approach Frank and I envisioned.

We spent the plane ride back from New York talking about the two schools. We were intrigued that equally successful programs could take place in such different settings—Dalton's multistoried traditional buildings in a dense urban neighborhood and Whitby's one-story contemporary school building on spacious suburban grounds. We compared their programs with another major influence on our thinking, the British Integrated Day program, which we had first encountered in Joseph Featherstone's seminal 1967 articles in the *New Republic*. Since even Frank couldn't justify flying to England, we had gathered additional information about this new British approach. We were both impressed with its key features— team teaching, multiage family grouping, an integrated yet flexible curriculum, and classrooms which provided space, materials, and furnishings for a variety of learning activities. The open, developmental approach we wanted for St. Francis, we decided, could best be implemented by combining features of the new British approach with aspects of progressive schools like Dalton and Whitby.

Frank had the good sense to know that no matter how sound his instincts and my analytic abilities were, as neophyte educators we needed some professional help. He hired Lovick Miller to spend a morning each week at St. Francis as consulting psychologist. Lovick was a Harvard-trained, Ph.D. clinical psychologist, and Director of the University of Louisville's Child Psychiatry Research Center. His easy-going manner was paired with a keen mind, superior training, and lots of experience. Lovick often provided helpful advice on handling problematic students. But his most important role was listening to Frank and me discuss the many provocative ideas we had accumulated about schools and kids. Every Wednesday morning, the three of us met in Frank's office. We would talk for an hour and a half about the school's organization, curriculum, facilities, students, teachers, parents, and policies. As an expert on child development, Lovick helped us be realistic. But he shared our excitement at having the opportunity to actually do, within reason, anything we believed would enhance learning. We three were equal participants in a lively, ongoing dialogue.

"Frank, I know you and Tom are enamored with multiage grouping, but imagine yourself a small, youngish five-year-old in one of these K-1-2 primary groups, with most of your classmates six or seven. Aren't you going to feel mentally and physically intimidated?"

"Not if the teacher gives you developmentally appropriate tasks," Frank responded. "You may be a precocious reader, better than most of the seven-year-olds, and will thrive in a reading group with your reading peers, whatever their age."

"Besides," I added, "think of the benefits of having older students as models of more mature behavior and learning attitudes."

"You two are such romantics," Lovick countered. "How do you keep the natural competitive drive from contaminating your educational Eden?"

"Come on, Lovick" I answered. "We are just as genetically designed for cooperation as for competition. It's the culture that has overemphasized competition."

"Before we get too far afield," said Frank, "I'll get some coffee. Then let's talk about how to evaluate readiness levels."

These discussions took place in the late 1960s, when the school was still located at St. Francis in the Fields Church. The school had been given fifty-five acres of rolling farmland in Goshen, eight miles east of the church and twenty miles from downtown Louisville. We were designing new facilities to replace the traditional classrooms we had shared with the church. We decided that an open floor plan would best facilitate the developmental programs we planned to implement and we hired an innovative local architect, Jasper Ward to design it. The result was a striking contemporary building that complemented the educational philosophy of the school.

The new facilities in Goshen were completed in the spring of 1970. Freed from the limitations posed by the church's spaces, we were finally able to implement the ideas we had been discussing ever since I had arrived in 1967. As a "school without walls," with multi-age groups and a progressive approach to learning, St. Francis School was unlike any school in Louisville. The genius of Jasper Ward's design was the way it created visual separation between instructional areas while maintaining the flexibility of an open plan. Within a few years of moving into the new facilities, the school was filled to capacity, attracting students from throughout the metropolitan area. When parents visited, they discovered, as Frank and I had at Dalton and Whitby, that engaged students paid little attention to visitors. Of course, there were prospective parents who could only imagine their children lined up in rows, receiving the same rote learning they had experienced. There were others who were disturbed by the movement and steady murmur of active learning. But for those parents who decided to enroll their children, many, in just a few weeks, would tell us how much their sons and daughters loved school, wanted to come each day, and seemed to be both learning and happy. Satisfied parents became the school's best marketing strategy. Their enthusiastic testimony was ultimately the most effective way to overcome resistance to how different St. Francis was from other Louisville schools.

Frank and I became advocates for student-centered learning, which involved both individual and cooperative activities and led to motivated, independent learners. We believed that all children and youth, unless severely mentally disabled, were capable of an academic education, but thrived best with a developmental approach. Confident of the school's program, we accepted a number of students who had not done well in traditional classrooms and succeeded with most of them. The key, almost always, was to provide developmentally appropriate expectations from teachers who were supportive, stimulating, and demanding. Finding and retaining such teachers was one of the most challenging and important parts of our jobs. Teachers with the skills and energy to work in student-centered schools like St. Francis were rare and often came from atypical backgrounds.

Sue Wood was from Hopkinsville, Frank's Western Kentucky hometown. Younger than Frank, she was a friend of Lucy Belle

Davidson, the school's receptionist, also from Hopkinsville. The year before the school moved out to Goshen, we needed a new lead teacher for one of the classes. Recently divorced, a single parent, Sue needed a job. While she had no teaching experience, she had a psychology degree and significant self-confidence. Frank correctly sensed that she had the makings of a first-rate teacher. Behind her Western Kentucky colloquialisms, Sue was bright, independent, stubborn, and unflappable. Unusual for someone who wanted to teach in the lower grades, she loved math. She and I both felt that math was the worst-taught subject in elementary schools, primarily because most elementary teachers were interested in reading, writing, and social studies. With my support, she was determined that St. Francis would be different. Manon Charbonneau, a teacher at an independent school in Cleveland, had pioneered a new, hands-on approach to mathematics. She used a mathematics laboratory—a specially equipped, designated space where students went regularly from their home classrooms. Sue attended one of Manon's summer workshops and came back a zealous convert. She immediately went to work to create a math lab program for St. Francis.

Whenever I went to the Lower School wing, I stopped at the Math Lab to watch Sue in action. The Lab was in the center of the Lower School, in between the primary and the third-fourth grade groups. Clusters of tables and chairs—surrounded by tall bright green and blue storage cabinets, some with chalkboards and bulletin boards— defined the octagonal Math Lab area, with spillover into the steps of the adjacent Lower School amphitheater. Several cabinets were full of marked bins containing a wide variety of colorful manipulative, "hands-on" materials—Cuisenaire Rods, peg boards, tangrams, pattern blocks, geoboards, rulers and compasses—the staples of an elementary mathematics laboratory. Other cabinets held bins of worksheets and student folders, one for each of the Lower School students.

I loved to sit on the amphitheater steps and watch a group of fifteen primary students, ages five to seven, come in for their math period. Sue welcomed them as they immediately went, without any instructions, directly to the bins, got their folders, picked up whatever materials they needed for the assignment they were working on, chose a workplace, and started to work. Sue was in constant motion and quiet conversation as she made personal contact with each student during the first five minutes. She checked her master sheet to confirm their activity choice, helped some students start a new activity, and quietly admonished others to step up their pace.

"Anne, why don't you do a set of geoboard problems next."

"Please, Ms. Wood, can I first do some tangram puzzles?"

"Sure, just make sure you start on geoboards tomorrow."

"Sam, I want this finished before you leave today. I have something new for you to start tomorrow. Let's move you over here to keep you from being distracted."

Her no-nonsense voice was a blend of encouragement and insistence as she gently moved him to a table by himself. Sam was one of our "risk" admissions. A brilliant, but hyperactive, distractible, and disorganized eight-year-old, he had continually disrupted the traditional classrooms at his previous school. Mathematically gifted, he could do complicated multiplication problems in his head. At his previous school he had refused to do the rote math worksheets, step by step, just like everyone else. He was exactly the kind of challenge Sue loved, and, in a few weeks, he became consistently productive. The concrete, manipulative materials kept him focused by requiring him to use both hands and brain to solve problems. Sam loved coming to the Lab, and Sue and his lead teachers worked out a special arrangement for him. If he finished his other work early, he could go work in the Math Lab.

Sue cajoled, kidded, directed, praised, corrected, and assisted her students, whatever it took to keep them engaged. As I observed students at work, maybe two of them were working at the same level on similar activities. The rest were doing different things at their individual readiness and achievement levels. Within Sue's continuum of math skills and concept development was the flexibility to move students at different rates along different paths, depending on their interests and learning styles. Similar in many ways to the Montessori approach, Sue's program, while equally developmental, had greater flexibility and included more group activities.

In the Middle School wing was a math teacher as outstanding with older kids as Sue was with five to nine year-olds. Walt Gander had an interactive style, which somehow magically connected with virtually every student in a class, regardless of their interest or ability in math. Tall and lean, looking like the basketball player he was, Walt was passionate about math and kids. He ran on high energy and an enthusiasm that engaged students. He loved the challenge of reaching those who said they hated math and claimed they couldn't do it. He would insist, even more vehemently, that they could, then sit down next to them and show them how. Walt had the rare gift of coming up with the perfect explanation for each student, instantly, hardly pausing to think. He personalized expectations by converting each course into a series of worksheets with which he could adjust pace and difficulty to fit the needs of individual learners. I would go into his class and watch him bounce back and forth from one student to another. He found time for everyone because of his uncanny ability to quickly diagnose a student's difficulty and respond with just the right cue.

Walt was without pretense and totally at ease with kids, especially middle- and high school students. His loves were teaching math and playing basketball and four-square. At school, he preferred the company of students and, when he had a free period, would invariably be in his classroom giving a couple of them extra help. During the mid-morning and lunch recess, weather permitting, Walt was outside playing four-square, a compact game where several agile, energetic thirteen-year-olds occasionally overcame his height and reach to win a couple of games, an exciting outcome for everyone including Walt. One student from the mid-1970s remembered three things particularly about Walt Gander: "the primitive computer that we programmed to calculate pi; the Volkswagen Beetle that I never understood how he fit inside; his response whenever we caught a mistake on the blackboard—'Just testing you to see if you're paying attention.'"

While a good developmental school can meet the needs of a wide range of student abilities and learning styles, there were a few students whose needs could not be met by St. Francis. Both they and the school would have benefited by our realizing this earlier, finding a better school placement for them, and insisting that they transfer. Two students come to mind, both determined to be disruptive, and neither the usual consequences nor peer pressure succeeded in changing their behavior. As much as Frank and I supported idiosyncratic kids, we learned that the school could not tolerate behavior that distracted the learning of other students.

What the two of us had most in common was deep respect and compassion for the young. We believed that within each child was the potential to be healthy, to be moral, to be productive, and to learn from mistakes. The essential Quaker belief that each of us has the divine, the sacred within us, is at the heart of both St. Francis Schools. In our personal interactions with young people, we sought to convey this belief, not just with words, but with empathy and compassion.

Frank Cayce and I had something else in common—a resistance to growing up and joining the adult world. A part of Frank was always childlike—playful and occasionally irresponsible, personally and fiscally. There is part of me that remains an adolescent—risk-taking, individualistic, and occasionally impulsive—and continues to respond to those impulses in my students. Joining the adult world meant for us limiting choices, excluding interests. I had already experimented with being a teacher, an engineer, an urban planner, and a philosopher. I learned that each profession required me to spend the working day too narrowly focused. Frank and I both discovered, almost by accident, that being administrators of a small, independent school gave us a venue in which we could deploy diverse and eclectic interests.

Frank and I had differences beyond his outgoing nature and my reserve. For all his creative ideas, Frank typically left the details of implementation to me and, over the years, I became impatient in his shadow, doing more of the detail work. But it took the two of us to establish St. Francis School and the school's success was too important to me and its students not to keep working hard and supporting Frank. I knew my calling was eventually to manage a small, independent school, preferably a high school, and I knew I was acquiring the skills needed.

Frank was a great storyteller and an excellent writer. His monthly newsletters to parents and friends of the school were creative and informative, not the typical headmaster reports. A good editor as well, he taught me to simplify my cumbersome sentences. He successfully removed "very" from my vocabulary by convincing me that its use weakened rather than strengthened the adjective it modified. I encouraged Frank to write about his life, especially his experiences as an educator. Sadly, he never found the energy and motivation to write his story, a loss to all of us who cared about him and the school.

During his last few years at St. Francis, Frank struggled with cancer. He was in the hospital for several long stretches of time, almost dying at one point. I was left to do two jobs and when he was able to come back, I continued to do part of his. The burden became increasingly onerous, and I finally confronted him in what was a sad, painful meeting for both of us. We were in his office, which looked out over the front courtyard of the school. Through his big window, we could see the forty-foot abacus with its bright blue and green beads, the school's logo, a symbol of hands-on learning. As far as we knew, it was the world's largest and most expensive abacus. Frank's insistence on building it was classic Frank Cayce. Some Board members called it "Frank's Folly," and it shows up to this day on webpages of "Roadside Attractions," but it distinctly marked the entrance of St. Francis School.

Frank was sitting on his couch; I was in a nearby chair. His two bouts with cancer had physically aged him. With strong emotion, but in my usual measured voice, I expressed my increasing frustration.

"I'm worn out by the extra time and energy it takes, doing some of your job as well as my own, and it's hard on me and my family."

"Tom, you know how tight the budget is. I can't ask the Board of Directors for additional help," he replied in a tired voice.

"I only know that I can't keep doing what I have been doing. I'm covering for you, Frank. It's not fair. If you won't talk to the Board, I will. They need to understand the situation."

"I'm sorry, but I'm tired and don't feel well most of the time. If you have to talk to the Board, go ahead; do what you need to do."

I left his office knowing he felt betrayed and that our relationship was irrevocably changed. The Board would ask him to resign as of the end of the year. They appointed me Acting Headmaster for the following school year, 1975-1976, and began a national search for a new headmaster.

Frank subsequently took a position as Chaplain at a Virginia boarding school and then returned to Louisville to become Rector of St. Andrew's Episcopal Church, retiring in 1983. When I would occasionally see him, we were cordial, but there was an ongoing, underlying discomfort between us. At the suggestion of several mutual friends, I visited him in the hospital not long before his death in July, 1992. Knowing Frank was terminally ill, I suspect that a catalyst in wanting to see him was that my father had died just two and a half months earlier. Frank, just four years younger than Pop, was more than a mentor to me. Pop was contained, emotionally constrained. From him I received the gift of competence and responsibility, from Frank, creativity and freedom.

Frank was in a private room at Norton Hospital, with a large window looking out over downtown Louisville. As I walked over from St. Francis High School, just a couple of blocks away, I thought about my years with him, realizing in a way I had not previously understood that the high school, my life's work, would not have existed without those eight years, including its frustrations. I loved this man and cherished the gifts he had given me.

He was propped up in bed, a book at his side as usual, the TV blessedly silent. While physically weak, his mind was fully alert. We had a lively, heartfelt conversation, sharing memories of working together. We reminisced about a week in 1969, when we spent five days downtown with the St. Francis School eighth grade, learning about urban environments. We held school in the city with academic classes in the morning coordinated with field trips in small groups during the rest of the day. Frank and I laughed as we remembered addressing a number of parental concerns about safety in "dangerous downtown." What had been a controversial extended field trip became one of the inspirations for my establishing St. Francis High School as an urban school. Frank told me how proud he was of what I had accomplished with the high school. I was able to tell him how much I had learned from him and what fun it had been developing St. Francis School together in the fields of Goshen.

Shortly after his father's death, Gordon Cayce wrote a piece about Frank's educational philosophy, published in the October 1992 *The Abacus*.

The final ingredients in this powerful new approach to learning were perhaps the most important. These were action and spontaneity. You could not wait around for things to happen, you had to be ready to try…. Trying something and failing could frequently teach you as much, if not more, than easy success. And if you did fail, the school would be there for you when you tried again. Lastly, spontaneity was the wild card thrown in to keep everyone on their toes…. One had to learn to "roll with the punches" in order to succeed in life. Life, by nature, is full of interruptions…. My father considered St. Francis School the highpoint of his life. It was one of those random moments of synchronicity when the right person shows up at the right place at precisely the right time.

Spontaneity—what a rare ingredient in schools and yet so central in children's behavior. I can see Frank, holding that wild, colorful mask, exclaiming "Fools Friday! Fools Friday!" as he threw open classroom doors.

# 4

## THIRD AND BROADWAY

I never felt more frustrated than one afternoon in February, 1977, during the few short months between board approval of the plan for the new St. Francis High School that past October and when we had to be ready to open in August. Board Chair Ken Reutlinger, Jr., and I were meeting with potential backers of the school—local banks, corporations, foundations, and individuals—asking them to contribute start-up money. A successful real estate broker, Ken was an accomplished salesman with a direct, can-do approach. He was big and a big talker; I was slight and a thinker. Together we developed what we believed was a persuasive presentation. I addressed the unique philosophy, goals, and programs of the new school. He spoke as a parent who wanted his two teenage children, Lee and Kenny, to have an alternative to the existing public and private high schools in Louisville. St. Francis was scheduled to open in eight months and the Board of Directors and I were worried about having sufficient funds to pay bills already accumulating. Initial payments were due on furnishings for the science labs and for kitchen equipment, two of the most expensive components of the new school's facilities.

While most people we approached seemed genuinely interested in what we were doing, money was slow to come in. We especially encountered scepticism about the school's location, which to us was essential, but to many others back in 1977 was an idea they simply couldn't grasp. "You're making a mistake," one potential backer assured us politely but firmly. "A downtown private school will never work." The negative responses did not discourage us; instead, they made us even more determined to succeed. We were convinced that an urban school made sense.

The committee's report to the St. Francis High School Board of Directors in March, 1976, had concluded that there was indeed sufficient demand among parents to support a new unit which would apply a progressive, student-centered philosophy to a college preparatory secondary program. The report recommended a separate school designed for adolescents with its own location, perhaps downtown, rather than added to current facilities in Goshen, designed for kindergarten through eighth-grade students. The majority of the committee members agreed to serve as the nucleus of a founding board of directors and appointed me as headmaster to develop and lead the new high school. The committee requested that the current ninth grade at St. Francis School be dropped, which would provide both eighth and ninth-grade students to feed into the new school. The St. Francis School Board agreed, provided that a satisfactory operating plan for the high school was presented to the Board at its October meeting in seven months.

I was excited, optimistic, and determined. Between the end of June when I finished at St. Francis School and the October meeting, I had to create fund-raising, marketing, and operating plans, a school brochure, and a comprehensive curriculum guide, plus expand the new school's Board of Directors and find possible locations. Starting

July 1, I was paid $600 a month to work twenty hours a week developing the school. I had begun an M.Ed. graduate program at the University of Louisville with a grant that paid tuition and a modest stipend. My wife had begun practice as a child psychiatrist and her income could cover the rest of our expenses. The previous year had been the most stressful in our marriage and she was upset at my decision to start the high school. The time, energy, and concentration needed to found a school would certainly be hard on my family. But our children were well along in age, youngest daughter Lisa going into the sixth grade at St. Francis School and son David an eighth grader enthusiastically planning to join the first ninth grade at St. Francis High School. Our oldest daughters, Sarah and Cathy both attended boarding schools.

The founding Board of Directors was a diverse group—three-fourths parents of already committed students and one-fourth interested community leaders. The group included a bank president, an education professor, a philanthropist, two real estate brokers, a financial advisor, a former high school teacher, a grandparent, a builder/developer, and the Dean of the Episcopal cathedral four blocks from the school's eventual site. While all were supportive, they peppered meetings with questions about what we were doing. Each meeting was an opportunity to promote the school's philosophy and goals. Since we were starting a school unlike any they or I had experienced, I often felt something like Moses leading the Israelites to the Promised Land. Ken later recalled, "There is nobody on the face of the earth more calmly determined to make something happen than Tom Pike. I was the first chairman of the board ... and I can tell you it was an uphill climb. But we marched on and never wavered."

Convincing this group, most of whom lived in the suburbs, that the new school should be located downtown was the first of many challenges. Sure, some of them worked in the city, but they had never considered sending their teenage children to an urban school.

For me, educational philosophy dictated placing St. Francis High School in the center of Louisville. Identity formation is the central task of adolescence. Traditional high schools fail to accomplish this critical task with the majority of students, partly because of their isolation from the adult world—its culture, commerce, and governance. These are the years when adolescents need to see themselves as independent, young adults. Their education needs direct, daily contact with the world they are being prepared to enter.

The personal and intellectual skills needed for success as an adult are no different from the skills needed for success in college. St. Francis High School's programs and courses would address the expectations of the workplace and the expectations of a classic liberal arts curriculum. Its students would be better prepared for both college and life than their peers from traditional college preparatory schools. Being downtown would facilitate the accomplishment of both objectives.

In July 1976, the Board reached consensus and approved the downtown location. I drafted text for a brochure, worked on a development plan and curriculum, and began the search for a suitable site. In September, Ken and I signed a fifteen-year lease and renovation agreement for space in the former YMCA Building at Third Street and Broadway.

Practical reasons for being downtown became obvious. By locating in an old building in the process of being renovated and seeking tenants, the costs of renovation would be absorbed over the life of the lease. The school's only responsibility was to equip and furnish the new facilities for a total start-up cost of $60,000. The school's library? Easy, the main branch of the city's library, well-stocked and staffed at no cost to the school, was across the street. Another plus of being in the old YMCA building was sharing athletic facilities with the newly opened Downtown Athletic Club, giving students and staff the use of a gym, pool, and fitness rooms.

A nearby city park provided playing fields and courts for school teams. School buses? We expected many students would ride public TARC (Transit Authority of River City) buses to school, since our Third and Broadway location was on or near major routes. The city's governmental offices, courts, museums, medical center, art galleries, theaters, colleges and universities were close by. Students and faculty could easily use these resources for community service, research projects, and internships. The school had its own kitchen used initially for food service from a nearby deli and then for the St. Francis Coop, a unique faculty/student-run lunch program. Coop members received discounted lunch prices in exchange for helping serve and clean up. Students also took advantage of the many restaurants within walking distance.

With facilities secured and a modest brochure describing the philosophy and goals ready for the printer, the next challenge was to have St. Francis School accept the high school's operating plan and agree to phase out its ninth grade. In October, a financial advisor whose daughter would be in the high school's first ninth grade, put together a comprehensive presentation. The St. Francis School trustees were impressed with the thoroughness of the plan and a majority approved it. We were now ready to actively recruit new students and mailings were made to parents of current seventh, eighth, and ninth grade students. On November 5, 1976, a press conference was held on the front steps of the historic building. This was the official kickoff for St. Francis High School. I noted in my journal: "I feel optimistic. There seems to be momentum that will ensure we get off the ground." Now began a ten-month countdown to the opening day of school, September 6, 1977—recruit students, hire teachers, raise money, and construct and furnish new facilities.

It was a challenge to convince parents to send their daughters and sons downtown to a small, unproven new high school located in a funky old YMCA building. But becoming an independent young adult by learning to manage oneself in a city environment has always been part of St. Francis' comprehensive approach to preparation for college and adult life. Ken enjoyed telling humorous stories about his daughter Lee, who started in the ninth grade in 1980. Lee invited Ken to have lunch at the McDonald's next door to the school. "There's a friend I want you to meet," Lee told him. "Her name is Katherine." At the appointed time, Ken met Lee at McDonald's and they sat down. "Here she comes," Lee said. Ken looked up to see a smiling homeless woman coming toward them, carrying bags containing her worldly possessions. Katherine had arrived. Not all parents had Ken's confidence in their teenage children. Virtually every prospective parent was concerned about downtown safety. We also had no football team, no cheerleaders, and no campus. We had yet to establish a college admissions record. But we were certain that if we delivered first-rate teachers, a rigorous academic program, and personal attention, parents would support this ambitious experiment.

While lots of time was spent meeting with prospective families, raising money, overseeing the building renovation, and developing the curriculum, the most important task was finding outstanding teachers—the best way to establish our reputation and overcome parental concerns about the controversial aspects of the school. Recruiting nationally and locally, I looked for well-educated, experienced people with varied backgrounds, keen knowledge of their subjects, and a desire to work personally with adolescents in a small school setting. I began interviewing in February and finally filled all positions in early August, just a month before school started. All eight of the full-time teachers had advanced degrees. Four relocated to Louisville from other parts of the country. Several part-time teachers completed the faculty. Of the dozen, a third had university teaching experience, a third came from independent schools, and the other third from public schools.

Attracted by the school's 8:1 student-teacher ratio, no bureaucracy, and unique philosophy and goals, the new faculty was talented and diverse: our first science teacher had earned her Ph.D. from McGill University in Canada, where she lived and taught before moving to Louisville. Her combination laboratory-classroom reminded me of a cross between a disorganized greenhouse and a messy kitchen, her once-white lab coat a multicolored collage of experiential stains.

For thirty-five years a member of Vassar College's English Department, Caroline Mercer, a small, lively, gray-haired professor, had an amazing mastery of literature stored in her acute mind. She used to tell the students stories about her good friend Eudora Welty. Caroline was the spryest seventy-year-old I had ever met and, surprisingly, one of the teachers most open to innovative programs.

Dan Beaufort, at twenty-four the youngest teacher, had taught English for three years at the public high school in the small town of Maysville in northeastern Kentucky. A Louisville native, he had heard about the new high school and asked to meet with me. We quickly discovered a shared enthusiasm and commitment for working in creative and supportive ways with teenagers. I offered him a part-time English position, which Dan accepted on the condition that he could work full-time for his part-time salary, doing whatever else would help establish the school.

Fran Donnelly, Spanish teacher and college counselor, heard about us while attending nearby Calvary Church. "I bumped into Burrell Farnsley, who suggested that I look into the newly founded urban school. Through a search engine, I learned of three possibilities: one in Surrey, England, one in Burbank, CA and one in Louisville, KY. I interviewed with Tom at Christ Church under the Bishop's portrait and then took a tour of a gutted shell of a building and learned of Tom's plans. I had to use my imagination with how the building/facilities would look, but Tom's educational vision was crystal clear. I was sold! When my sister joined the faculty in 1986, she was equally eager to become a part of the St Francis Community that

Tom built. We may be the only siblings who worked there together." They were. Fran ended up staying even longer than I did.

Jim Hurst, a young Episcopal priest with an English degree from Duke University, was teaching English and Social Studies at St. Francis School in Goshen and was also an excellent athlete. I looked forward to his teaching, coaching, and developing two original courses: Exploring Human Nature for ninth graders and Transition for the seniors. With beard and long hair, looking like the stereotypical Jesus of Nazareth, Jim was an outspoken advocate for the ordination of women in a community where the majority of Christians were opposed to women being ministers. At the March 1977 meeting of the Board of Directors, I alerted the Board that hiring Jim might adversely affect enrollment and donations, both of which were behind schedule. Board member Eleanor Norman, a grandparent, lifelong Episcopalian, fabric artist, and unusually progressive for her generation, spoke up. "Jim Hurst's views on women's ordination are his personal views, which he is free to express. He's not speaking for the school. Besides, as the only coeducational private high school in Louisville, St. Francis is committed to equal treatment of boys and girls." I was never sure how many Board members actually agreed with Eleanor or simply deferred to a prominent elder, but her response settled the matter. Several other Board members expressed appreciation for my open and direct manner which established a pattern of openness and trust with this and subsequent Boards of Directors.

The school's first brochure stated that "The heart of a good school is its faculty. Their skill and concern are ultimately the only guarantee of effective learning." The founding faculty provided that guarantee in abundance. Not everyone worked out, and some, like Caroline, were already near retirement. But Fran Donnelly was still at St. Francis when I retired in 2003, as was Tim Marshall, who first joined us as a soccer coach in 1980. Dan, Jim, English teacher Neil

McCullough, and Art teacher Ellen Warden would stay from the beginning for many years, helping me to mold and grow the school.

In May, only four months before the start of school, difficulties arose with the Kentucky Department of Education. For credibility with prospective parents and to meet college admissions expectations, the new school had to be accredited, meeting the requirements for Kentucky high schools, public and private. Not surprisingly, we didn't, as St. Francis was deliberately designed to be different. One of the bureaucrats assigned to accredit nonpublic schools was a jolly, bald, good-old-boy state functionary, who loved to tell stories and eat good food. Over several long lunches at the fashionable downtown Brown Hotel, he helped us through the accreditation process.

One requirement was that high schools have a library with so many books per student. Other than basic reference books, we had planned for St. Francis students to use the main branch of the Louisville Free Public Library, right across the street from the school. I explained:

"It makes no sense to spend money on hundreds of books. The city's library has over a million books, many times more than any high school library in Kentucky. That's one reason we chose this location. I know the city's library is not actually part of our facilities, but it's only eighty yards away."

"I know what we can do." He began thinking out loud. "The regulation's purpose is to ensure that students have ready access to a basic library collection. The libraries in most big public high schools are more than eighty yards from many of their students. I can pass you."

Another hurdle was that high schools in Kentucky were required to have fifty-five minute class periods. I had planned a flexible schedule, with more periods in a school day, mostly forty minutes long, with double periods on some days for art and science labs. The state wanted six periods, each fifty-five minutes long.

I argued that St. Francis' small classes of fifteen students could easily learn in forty minutes what classes of thirty learn in fifty-five minutes in public schools.

"That makes sense to me. I can give you a waiver on that requirement, too." And so the visit went, and the school received its accreditation.

The major crisis came in early June. School was scheduled to open in three months; the majority of teachers were under contract; construction of facilities was on schedule; equipment and furnishings had been ordered, but both enrollment and fundraising were behind schedule. We had neither sufficient students nor enough money to start the school. At a tense Board of Directors' meeting, bank president Maury Johnson spoke, "If you can't raise the money, what is your backup plan?" I quietly and firmly answered, "There are no alternative plans. The school will open as scheduled." Maury helped the school obtain the necessary line of credit to cover the projected shortfall. The Louisville *Courier-Journal* helped out by publishing a timely article in June. The newspaper's owner had long supported St. Francis, and the editorial editor's son was an incoming freshman at the high school. But the main reason they ran the story, long-time editor Keith Runyon told me recently, was "because SFHS was going to be a player in downtown. Which it has remained!!" Admissions inquiries picked up and more students enrolled. By the start of school, there were sixty students, the minimum number needed to maintain our credit.

Later in June, to obtain two of those first sixty students, it was necessary to take on the U.S. Department of Justice's Immigration Office. Mr. Sharudhi, an Iranian immigrant living in Louisville, had sought admission for two Iranian teenagers, Afsanah and Hamid Esanzadeh, children of friends still living in Iran. We found an impartial speaker of Farsi to translate their school records, but they needed student visas. Long waits, both on the phone and at the immigration office, were normal. Getting action taken or discovering the status of actions seemed impossible. Time was running out when we contacted Congressman Ron Mazzoli, whom I knew slightly. He helped us obtain the necessary papers and Hamid and Afsanah arrived just in time for the start of school, adding an international element to the new student body. An unexpected bonus was Hamid's skill at soccer, a great help to the school's new team in competing against older, more experienced players.

At the first staff meeting a week before the opening of school, teachers were concerned that there was not yet a class schedule, that the bathrooms lacked mirrors and partitions, and that the math books had not arrived. "But it was just electric," remembers Fran. "Everyone knew they were creating something different and exciting. We all came in with such energy."

An urban orientation was planned for the first two days of school. Students and teachers met in the Commons Room to start the opening day together with a moment of silence and to share announcements and concerns. "Morning Meeting" became a St. Francis tradition. After making a few welcoming comments and introducing the faculty and staff, I turned the meeting over to Mayor Harvey Sloane, a strong supporter of the school, who officially welcomed everyone to the city. Historian Tom Owen gave a talk, "Louisville History in a Nutshell," and showed an Al Shands film, "Time Remembered," the first of three we would see throughout the day, depicting Louisville's history from its founding in 1778. Al's award-winning films were crafted from drawings, paintings, still photographs, movie clips, and period music.

On our urban expedition we walked in small groups down to Main Street next to the Ohio River and engaged in an information scavenger hunt on the way. After taking tours of the area with guides from Preservation Alliance, we had lunch in the Stairways Building on historic Main and then walked back to the school for a tour of the new facilities. Several pedestrians, wondering why high school students were wandering the streets, asked us who we were. I proudly identified my students and staff with, "We're from St. Francis High School, the new school at Third and Broadway."

The next day we went south to Old Louisville, a Victorian-era residential area next to Louisville's Central Park. After a picnic lunch at a downtown park, we visited City Hall and met in the Aldermanic Chambers. After touring five of Louisville's new skyscrapers, we returned to the school for a briefing on the beginning of classes the next day. During the two-day immersion into the urban environment students and teachers regrouped several times to become acquainted with each other.

As I wandered through the school on opening day, helping students find their classes, observing activities, and talking with teachers and students, energy and enthusiasm permeated the halls and classrooms. While exhausted, I felt enormous relief. Interacting with students those first few days confirmed my calling to work among adolescents. But I had no idea what that work would look like or that I would stay for twenty-six years.

# 5

## TREE OF LIFE

Near the end of a school day one May, three students, together with their art teacher, came to the school office and asked to see me. They brought into my office what appeared to be a large framed picture wrapped in brown paper. Pam was carrying the package, accompanied by classmates Paul and Anne. I knew that the art classes had gone the day before to Louisville's J. B. Speed Art Museum to buy an original work of art from the purchase gallery for the school's hallways. Teacher Ellen Warden's idea was to use the selection process to put her students in the role of art critic. As the school's first art teacher Ellen was a persistent advocate of art as equally important to St. Francis's curriculum as science, math, English, history, and foreign languages. Her influence is still present four decades later as all students continue to be required to take a year long studio art course. Instructors are practicing artists, Artists-in-Residence, and art classes have double periods. Throughout her fourteen years at St. Francis, Ellen's strong voice was also insistent that women be equally affirmed and represented in every aspect of school life.

Pam, Paul, and Anne had gone to the Speed Museum earlier that week to narrow down the possible choices for purchase. They were obviously pleased with this year's selection and wanted to show me what the students had picked.

"Sit down, Mr. Pike," Pam said excitedly. "We thought you better have a look at what we bought yesterday before we hang it in the hallway. It's called "Tree of Life," by Brian Talley, a local artist. It was the first choice of the majority of art students, but it may be objectionable to other students and some teachers and parents."

They unwrapped the picture, a striking, skillfully executed sketch of a nude woman, black ink on white paper. They described the lively discussion which took place among the art students regarding the merits of the piece and its appropriateness as part of St. Francis' publicly displayed art collection. I was impressed with the responsible way they handled the selection of a controversial choice from a dozen nominated pieces. To their relief, I supported their decision.

The picture was hung first in the Commons Room and then in the main hallway. I did not view the picture as pornographic or offensive. A petition did circulate throughout the school for several weeks objecting to its purchase and expressing concern that some people, especially parents of prospective students, might be offended by the picture and have a negative impression of the school. But "Tree of Life" was an important symbol of the decision-making at St. Francis, a tangible example of the involvement of students in school policies which affect them, a St. Francis tradition. As one teacher said, "Those of us here love it; it's an extension of the philosophy of the school."

Four years later, I stepped out of the elevator on the third floor early one morning and the wall where "Tree of Life" had hung was empty. It had disappeared. At Morning Meeting that day, I gave a brief history of the picture, described the controversy and debate its purchase had caused, and made a plea for its return. Unfortunately it never reappeared and those of us who remember the vital discussion surrounding its acquisition consider the loss of the picture the theft of an important part of the school's history.

# 6

## SUDDEN DEATH

When I arrived at school on an October morning in 1980, Becky, a ninth grader, saw me come out of the elevator and walked up to me with tears in her eyes. Her voice shaking, she told me that Kurt had shot himself last night. His brother found him unconscious in his room and called EMS, but Kurt died several hours later at University Hospital.

As I absorbed her message, I struggled to find words to respond to her grief. She and Kurt had been close friends ever since they were students together at St. Francis School. I told her how sorry I was and how much I admired the ways that she and her classmates had supported his struggles as a disabled kid who was also the only African American in his class and one of only four in the school.

Quickly, I called Kurt's home. His aunt answered the phone and confirmed what had happened. I asked my secretary Brenda to put a note about Kurt's death in each staff member's mailbox, informing them also of a modified class schedule which I would announce at Morning Meeting. I instructed her to refer all phone calls from parents and the news media directly to me and to tell Jim Hurst to come immediately to my office.

Sitting at my desk, I began to address the many thoughts and feelings flooding into awareness. I had twenty minutes before Morning Meeting, the all-school assembly which started each school day. Sudden, unexpected deaths of adolescents have a profound, traumatic impact on a high school community, especially in a small school. Some of Kurt's classmates had known him since they were in kindergarten together at St. Francis School in Goshen. We were just a month into St. Francis High School's fourth year and I knew that students, parents, and staff would need both immediate and ongoing support.

I had already dealt with one suicide two years earlier, my first as leader of a school. The logistics of starting a new high school had been easy for my problem-solving mind. But in 1978, when Stuart, a tenth-grader, asphyxiated himself and was found dead the next morning, I was totally unprepared to deal with the emotional impact of a student's suicide. While many aspects of the current suicide were different from the earlier one, I was determined not to repeat the mistakes I had made in 1978. My response had been defensive and aloof during a sad, difficult period. I still felt badly about my poor handling of that first sudden death.

Looking back, Stuart's death felt harder to explain. Both young men had been popular and personable, but as son of a prominent white Louisville family, Stuart's harder-to-fathom depression seemed to me a world away from Kurt's visible differences. We always feel responsible when someone close to us takes their life, but because Kurt was Black and disabled, we somehow felt more personally responsible. This may not have been rational or fair as a judgment, but this was how I and others felt at the time. This time I would be both decisive and supportive.

Jim Hurst came in. Friend, colleague, and priest, Jim had training in counseling and crisis management. We had worked together after the previous suicide; he would help me with this one, and hopefully we would do better. In the few minutes before Morning Meeting, we planned a special schedule for an unusual school day.

Jim and I went across the hall through the double doors into the Commons Room, a large corner room on the third floor. Students and teachers were sitting at tables, on benches along the walls, on the carpeted floor. The news of Kurt's suicide had already spread and, as the bright morning sun streamed through the many windows, the school community talked quietly, a few crying students being consoled by friends. I convened the Morning Meeting with my usual words, "Quiet please, quiet," then began the meeting with the customary moment of silence. I announced Kurt's death, said a few words about his courageous struggle since birth with the crippling effects of cerebral palsy, and stated that the start of classes was postponed until 9:45, with a special schedule of shortened class periods for the balance of the school day. Once other announcements were made, we all walked to Calvary Church a block away on Fourth Street. We had done this in 1978 after the earlier suicide: being in a nearby, quiet place of sanctuary had felt comforting. Just as they respond to spontaneous surprise, teenagers respond to spiritual space outside of the daily routine. Jim spoke for a few minutes about Kurt, about death, and about suicide. An extended period of quiet followed—a time to individually begin to absorb what had happened. After returning to the school, students had a half hour break to talk with friends or staff members, who were available in classrooms and offices. The abbreviated class schedule then ran its course to the end of the school day at 3:00. Teachers were asked to give Jim or me the names of any students who seemed especially disturbed about Kurt's death. Also, any student who felt too upset to attend classes would not just be excused, but brought to the office to talk with Jim. If necessary, he would contact parents to come take the student home.

Back in my office, I located the file I had compiled during the aftermath of the earlier suicide, almost exactly two years before. I needed to draft a staff memo and a parent letter containing important suicide-prevention information. In the process, I would refresh my own memory. Not surprisingly, I remembered just about everything about the data around suicide:

Depression and/or feelings of hopelessness are the most important factors in suicide.

Around 50% of high school students report having thoughts about suicide.

Many teenagers who take their own lives declare their intention in some way. They may tell friends they are thinking about suicide or have already made an attempt. They will almost always ask them not to tell anyone, which can later cause the friends intense feelings of guilt.

Suicide attempts of any kind should always be considered a "cry for help."

The use of alcohol or other drugs is often a contributing factor. Such use can lower inhibitions, impair judgment, and aggravate other risk factors.

Deaths from suicide cause an intense, complex set of emotions including grief, anguish, guilt, and anger.

Girls are three times as likely to attempt suicide, but boys three

times more likely to succeed, primarily because boys tend
to choose guns or hang themselves whereas girls usually
take pills.

With feelings of guilt and sadness, my consciousness was pierced
by the image of a smiling Kurt on crutches, his withered legs in
heavy braces, greeting his many friends as he maneuvered his slight
body down the hall to another class. I felt guilty because Kurt had
not been a strong student and had struggled to meet the expectations
of the college preparatory courses at St. Francis. The Admissions
Committee had been impressed with his motivation but hadn't
been sure he could make it academically, especially in the required
math courses. But he and his parents were determined that he have
the chance, so we agreed and accepted him. Had we put him in an
untenable position, set him up for failure?

The sadness came from learning earlier that day that Kurt had
been depressed and why. Kurt's main source of pleasure came from
the many friends he had gained through his sense of humor and
good nature. I knew he was discouraged about grades, but I had
forgotten about his being a sexually mature fifteen-year-old male.
On the way back from the church one of his close friends, Laurie,
told me that Kurt had become despondent, believing that his crippled
body, his being on crutches, would keep him from ever having a real
girlfriend. She had never expected Kurt to commit suicide, but felt
guilty about not telling anyone how depressed he was. I assured her
she had been a wonderful, supportive friend to Kurt ever since they
were in first grade together.

I knew that Laurie and other friends of Kurt wanted to go see his
parents that afternoon and I promised her to arrange the visit. After
school, Jim and I took Laurie and nine other of Kurt's classmates to
his house. The students, while subdued, were remarkably sensitive
and articulate in conveying their admiration and affection for Kurt to

his parents and brothers. I was proud of them. When I was fourteen I certainly lacked the maturity and confidence to console the grieving family of a dead classmate.

Sudden deaths of teenagers, whether from suicide, illness, or accident, impact the entire school community, not just friends of the dead student and their parents. Everyone is jarred, caught up short. We think, "It could have been my friend, my child, my student, even me." It is especially traumatic for teenagers, who typically are "temporally provincial": they live in the present. They think they are immortal; most of them have not experienced human death, perhaps pets, but not humans. Sure people die, but "that's old people." They may know of teenagers who have been killed in an accident or died of an illness, but that's not going to happen to them. When they wake up one morning and arrive at school to learn that Stuart had poisoned himself with carbon monoxide or Kurt had shot himself, they are in disbelief. When they hear that he died shortly after arriving unconscious at the hospital, they are numb. Someone who has always been part of their school, whether for a month or since kindergarten, is no longer there. The dependable world of their present existence has been shattered. This jolt, the deconstruction of their reality, is deeply unsettling. They gather together, keep together, hug a lot, talk a lot. While they will respond to adults, they reach out to each other more, because adults with their years of experience don't share the same acute feelings about what happened.

I recently talked about Kurt with his Spanish teacher, Fran Donnelly. She remembers that Kurt's Spanish class was scheduled to attend a Ballet Folklórico performance. The day before he shot himself he had returned his ticket to her saying that he wouldn't be able to go. She was puzzled at the time, but didn't question him. "Obviously, he had already planned his suicide," she concluded. While turning in his ticket seems an absurdity when planning to leave life, gestures like this are often part of adolescent suicides.

Kurt wanted to cause the least amount of trouble for the people he cared about.

There is always the danger that one suicide will trigger others, so adults must be alert to feelings of hopelessness and signs of depression. I was concerned that Kurt may have made his intentions known to one or more of his friends who would now be overwhelmed with guilt for not telling anyone. Another student, a senior, was distraught because not long before he had made a racist taunt at Kurt and felt responsible for his death. Three weeks after Kurt's death, two girls told a teacher they had heard two friends of theirs talking seriously about suicide. With the help of an experienced suicide counselor we were able to intervene and gradually defuse their despair.

The experience of the suicide of a friend or family member remains deeply imbedded in memory. To this day, a memorial painting by Ellen Warden hangs in the college counselor's office. And almost thirty years after Kurt's suicide, a classmate wrote me that she remembered seeing Kurt a couple of days before he died, at school, sitting in a chair with his head down, looking sad. "This was not like him. When we were at St. Francis School, it seemed like he was always laughing. He had the best laugh. But the biggest concern in my opinion was what he was up against—a black teenager, crippled with cerebral palsy, in an almost all-white high school." She recalled going to Kurt's home. "I remember the front of the house, the entryway, and Frances, Kurt's mother, talking with us. But, they are the briefest of scenes, like photographs. It is like a heavy veil has been thrown over that time. Decades later I still have not accepted what happened."

# 7

## SECOND CHANCES

"Steve is a good boy." Mr. Baumann told me. "He's quiet, maybe a bit immature, but he's never been in trouble before. He says that he took my revolver to school to impress his classmates. It wasn't loaded and he planned to keep it in his locker. I can't believe he was stupid enough to show it to another student. He needs to get back in school, but no school will take him when we tell them what he did."

I was in my office with two distraught parents, George and Mary Baumann. George was a third-generation painter in his family's business, founded in the 1890s by his German immigrant grandfather. He wore a suit coat over his white overalls and Mary had on a simple, belted fifties-style house dress. They hoped to enroll their son, a tenth grader, who had been expelled from the Brown School, a nearby downtown public magnet school. The classmate to whom he had shown the revolver told the principal about the gun. Even though it was unloaded and Steve had threatened no one, possessing a gun in Louisville's public schools brings automatic dismissal. His parents had not been able to find another high school that would enroll him.

I asked them about Steve, what kind of student he was, his personality traits, his interests. Mrs. Baumann spoke up in a soft voice. "Steve's a quiet, well-behaved boy. He's shy and as a teenager has had difficulty making friends. He seems lonely. But he's always been a good student and we had hoped he would be our first child to go to college."

I called Martha, the principal at Steve's school, whom I happened to know because the Brown School, also downtown a few blocks to the north, was at that time the only other progressive school in town. A gifted, gutsy woman, she and I shared many ideas about kids and learning. She told me that Steve was a normal, nice kid, but had a dumb idea about impressing some classmates. She would not have expelled him but had had no choice because the no guns rule allowed no exceptions. "Tom," she said, "the only risk in your accepting Steve will be adverse public relations."

Since its inception in 1977, St. Francis High School had accepted a number of transfer students from other high schools. Most had chosen to leave their former school, seeking a more stimulating and supportive academic environment. But some were told to leave, either for unsatisfactory academic performance or for violation of school rules. Adolescence is complex and sometimes turbulent, a time of experimentation during a period of immature judgment. Risky, impulsive, rule-breaking behaviors occasionally brought students and parents from other schools into my office, often as a last resort. In each situation, I learned as much as possible about the teenager as a person and as a student. Relying also on intuition, I would ask myself if this kid could be successful in St. Francis' unique programs.

I met with Steve, a reserved, pleasant boy, hair recently cut, and neatly dressed in pressed jeans and a checked sports shirt with a collar. He was immediately forthcoming and appropriately apologetic about the trouble his poor judgment has caused his parents. He looked straight at me and said, "You'll have no trouble with me, Mr. Pike. I would like to go to school here." This was an okay kid. I saw no reason why he would not be successful at St. Francis. However, I did need to think seriously about the potentially negative public relations implications of admitting him. As a relatively new independent school, St. Francis High School was already considered unconventional due to its downtown location and progressive philosophy and attracting sufficient new students was an ongoing challenge.

"I think you would do well at St. Francis, but I need to check with a couple of other people. I'll call your parents tomorrow."

After Steve left, I went over his file again, especially the notes from my conversation with Martha Ellison. She trusted Steve enough to recommend him to me. I trusted her judgment and honesty. Teenagers respond positively to expectations in a climate of trust. Loyalty is a strong trait of adolescence and teenagers are loath to let down adults who trust them. But impulsivity is another adolescent trait. As well-honed as my intuition was, could I risk the school's reputation and safety? I knew Steve's best chance for growth in maturity and judgment was for his teachers and classmates not to know what he had done. I also knew that the St. Francis Board of Directors, parents, and probably most of the teachers would be appalled if they learned he had brought a gun to school. And if not appalled, they would likely project onto Steve a shadow of suspicion which could sabotage his progress.

I decided to accept Steve, but told no one why he had left the Brown School. He needed a completely clean slate, a fresh start. I made a condition of his enrollment that neither Steve nor his parents tell anyone why he left. I instructed them instead to say that they felt he would do better in the smaller classes and more personalized setting at St. Francis. Saying yes to Steve Baumann was the most unusual and questionable time I accepted a student. Steve enrolled, was a satisfactory student, stayed out of trouble, and graduated without anyone finding out about the gun.

Looking back at this incident decades later, I marvel at the risk I took in accepting Steve and the confidence I had in my intuition about him. Had I been wrong, the potential public relations and legal consequences could have ruined the school. After the Heath and Columbine shootings in 1997 and 1999 and in a time of micromanaging, hovering parents, I'm not sure I could now risk making the decision I made in 1985.

During the construction of new facilities, a two-year process begun in 2000, Baumann Painters were hired to restore the ornate plaster details in a large meeting room down the hall from my temporary office. When I went to the office one morning, a worker came up to me. A now thirty-year-old Steve Baumann introduced himself. He had come back to Louisville from Colorado the previous year to join the company as a fourth-generation painter. Steve thanked me for letting him come to St. Francis when no other avenue was open to him. I told him I was glad it had worked out and that I appreciated his coming up and thanking me. He then surprised me.

"Mr. Pike, I want to pay the school back. I told my supervisor that he's not to pay me for the couple of weeks we work on this project. I asked him to subtract my wages from the School's bill. Consider it a gift to the scholarship fund."

"There's no need for you to do that."

"It's the least I can do for your taking a chance on me."

Being able to take chances with kids was one reason I started St. Francis High School.

# 8

## THE SIGN OUT POLICY

The St. Francis philosophy is to learn by doing. We learn the importance of kindness by doing community service and discover the significance of respect from the close teacher-student relationships we build. We discover the value of responsibility by having it: we have the sign-out policy.

*The Fresco*, St. Francis High School's student newspaper, October 1998

In November, 1993, Bill and Keith, both seniors, and Sam, a freshman, appeared before the Discipline Review Board for violating the school's sign-out policy. A teacher had seen them at Bill's car in the parking lot behind the Holiday Inn a block down Broadway from the school. Suspicious, she checked the sign-out sheets when she returned and discovered that the three boys had listed their destination as McDonald's next door to the school. Going to a place other than the location entered on the daily sheets is a serious violation of school policy and typically results in restriction of freedom for a designated period of time.

Sam, the ninth grader, was a bright, vocal, lively, socially active kid—a highly visible student, liked by both students and teachers. Bilingual, his mother Hispanic, he often tucked his dark hair under a black beret.

Keith was an average student, doing what was needed to get passing grades. He typically wore jeans and t-shirt, with long brown hair falling down his back and chest. He had been suspended the previous year for a major offense and his parents had responded by hiring a lawyer. After a series of tense meetings we reached a compromise: Keith was allowed to come back to school on probation, but I was allowed to make a public statement to St. Francis students and staff, holding Keith accountable.

Bill was a quiet, unexceptional teenager who avoided drawing attention to himself, one of those "under the radar" kids. Slim, his clothes were on the borderline between clean-cut and scruffy. Usually, his long blond hair was tied back in a ponytail.

When not attending classes, St. Francis students choose how and where to spend their open periods, including the option of leaving the school under specific guidelines. Discipline at St. Francis is enforced by an unusual two-tier student court system, first implemented in 1986. Minor offenses—being late to class or being disruptive—are handled directly by the staff. Serious offenses— cutting a class, disrupting learning, and major sign-out violations— require an appearance before the Discipline Review Board, which chooses penalties appropriate to the offense. The Discipline Review Board, a student jury, is key to the system. The DRB consists of eight students, chosen by lot, every six weeks, two from each grade. St. Francis students feel a sense of ownership and responsibility for the school's discipline system because they are central to its implementation.

The sign-out policy and the school's downtown location, both integral to St. Francis' mission, have been controversial since the school's inception. Prospective parents often ask about the risks of allowing students to go outside the building. Many parents of teenagers are fearful and protective and I respond with patience and reassurance. Yes, there have been a few incidents over the years. Jackie's wrist was broken from a fall caused by a turning car as she crossed Second Street. Evan was walking down the alley behind the Brown Hotel counting the bills in his wallet when it was grabbed from his hands. But I explain to parents that leaving the building to go across the street to the city's main library, to a coffee shop down the street, or to the bookstore around the corner is important preparation for navigating a college campus. I also tell them that, since the majority of St. Francis students are from suburban families, all new students receive a downtown orientation which includes basic safety precautions for being in an urban setting.

The sign-out policy works because St. Francis is a small school where students feel known and trusted. They value the freedom given them and know that they risk losing it if they are irresponsible. Their desire to retain sign-out privileges provides an incentive for appropriate behavior both inside and outside the school.

Two days after the three boys went to the Holiday Inn parking lot, the Discipline Review Board met to hear their case. Dean of Students Tim Marshall submitted an "Amicus Curiae Brief" to the DRB, something he rarely did. Universally admired and respected by students for his engaging and knowledgeable teaching of U.S. History, Tim was equally known for his ability to be both an advocate for students and an impartial enforcer of rules.

I feel compelled to write in this particular case because I believe that the sign-out privilege at St. Francis is sacrosanct and this offense against the system should be taken seriously.

It is hard to imagine St. Francis without this privilege, but in reality the privilege is always in a precarious position. Mr. Pike instituted the sign-out system against the prevailing winds of community opinion regarding adolescents and freedom/responsibility. These three students have not upheld the responsibility that goes along with the freedom. Such a violation of the system betrays trust. … I am particularly disappointed that such a cavalier attitude was exhibited by seniors.

Students turned in to the DRB have the option of appearing and defending themselves. Keith, Bill, and Sam claimed that they had gone to Bill's car to get his wallet before going to McDonald's. The DRB convicted them of a serious offense and sentenced them to the loss of sign-out privileges for two weeks. Irate, all three protested that their punishment was excessive. They also felt unjustly singled out by the Dean of Student's intervention and complained that Tim Marshall's brief had unfairly influenced the student jury.

While the DRB jury system worked remarkably well, an important change had become necessary two years earlier that would come into play with Keith, Bill, and Sam's case. In 1991, five years after the system had been implemented, Teresa, the school's receptionist, called me over the intercom.

"Tom, there's an agitated student here who needs to talk to you."

"Send him in," I replied. Kevin, a spacey, disheveled sophomore, flustered and distraught, came into my office.

"Have a seat, Kevin. What's going on?"

"It's the DRB, Mr. Pike. I forgot to sign in when I came back from lunch."

"Were there any other issues involved?"

"Well, it was the second time this quarter. I was in a big hurry so I wouldn't be late to class again. I expected to be grounded, maybe for a week, but the DRB grounded me for a whole month, which is way too long."

"That does sound a bit harsh."

"What can I do? There's no way to appeal an unfair penalty."

As this was the first time someone had formally complained about a DRB ruling, I asked the School Committee, St. Francis's student council, to propose an appeals process. After discussing Kevin's dilemma, everyone agreed that there should be a second, separate court for appeals brought by students or staff who felt that a DRB consequence was inappropriate, either too harsh or too lenient.

The new court, called the St. Francis Supreme Court, would have five members, four juniors and seniors elected by the student body, plus the Head of School as moderator and tiebreaker. Appeals would be submitted in writing and circulated among the five judges, who could either decide to hear the case or let the DRB ruling stand. The proposal was submitted to the school community and overwhelmingly approved. Judges were elected, Kevin submitted a written appeal, and the new court chose to hear his case. They ruled in his favor and reduced the period of grounding from a month to two weeks. This unique two-tier court system continues today to administer justice at St. Francis High School.

Two years later, not surprisingly, Bill, Keith, and Sam appealed to the Supreme Court.

> We request that the Supreme Court of St. Francis High School conduct a retrial regarding the incident of sign-out violations and visit to a student's car. ... We wish to appeal this conviction because we feel that the DRB's punishment is unreasonable and harsh. It appears that pressures from administration to make an example of us unfairly influenced the judgment. ... We simply request to have our case tried justly and for the punishment to reflect the seriousness of the offense. We feel

that if this case is tried in a detailed and considered manner, then the "serious offense" nature of our conviction will be altered. Thank you.

The Supreme Court chose to hear the appeal and convened two days later during lunch. Bill, who had written the appeal, presented their case. After hearing his explanation, the Court excused the three plaintiffs and began their deliberation. All four of the elected student members felt that the DRB conviction was proper and the punishment not excessive given the three boys' blatant violation of the sign-out rules. Several commented that the Dean of Students' unprecedented note to the DRB was unusual and perhaps impolitic. But they did not believe Tim's note had affected the DRB's decision.

One member suggested that this was a good opportunity to remind the school community of the unique importance of the sign-out system. He proposed that one of the ten days of grounding be replaced with the three boys being required to stand up in Morning Meeting, state what had happened, and apologize for putting the system in jeopardy. For some students, having to stand before the entire school community and apologize may be a more effective consequence than grounding. The Supreme Court unanimously affirmed the DRB's ruling as amended by the suggestion. Bill, Sam and Keith were not happy with the result, but made an acceptable presentation at Morning Meeting and served their nine days grounding.

Two days after the Supreme Court's decision I received a lengthy letter from Bill's parents about the harshness of their son's punishment, that "this process violates our sense of fairness and justice … the initial disciplinary action was excessively severe, particularly for a first offense, and that the punishment as amended, is just as excessively severe." They complained that the DRB had inadequate guidelines and further stated that staff members should not "intervene in individual cases at will." At the end of the letter, they announced their withdrawal of support of St. Francis—including a significant financial contribution and the father's participation on the Parents' Committee.

Parents need to support their children, but the letter irritated me. Bill was treated fairly and given a typical penalty, even for a first offense. Tim and I suspected that the boys went to Bill's car for a drug deal. We were having issues with drugs at the time and there had been an incident the previous year with one of the other boys. But in this case we had no evidence and, while frustrated, chose not to voice our suspicions to the courts or to the parents. The boys might have been innocent, except for the sign-out violation.

When I went back to the yearbook to find out more about Bill, there was little to learn. During his four years at St. Francis, he was an average, but successful student, belonged to the guitar club, and did his required community service at the Louisville Zoo.

But Bill's senior yearbook page was a total surprise, unlike any other senior's page. Instead of the usual collage of photos and quotations from song lyrics and favorite authors, the sole content of Bill's page was his name at the top and a thirty-seven-line quote from Franz Kafka's novel, *The Trial*. The page was completely covered by thirty-eight closely spaced lines of text. I would never have imagined Bill reading Kafka, much less using Kafka's words to make a unique protest on his senior page. Clearly, he still felt strongly about the punishment given for violating the sign-out policy. And I had forgotten that he had written the appeal to the St. Francis Supreme Court and appeared before the court to argue his, Keith's, and Sam's case.

The excerpt is from the next to last chapter, "In the Cathedral," where the prison chaplain tells Joseph K., *The Trial*'s central character, that his case is going badly.

"You are held to be guilty. ... Your guilt is supposed, for the present, at least, to be proved."

"But I am not guilty," said K.; "it's a misunderstanding. ..."

"You are deluding yourself about the Court," said the priest and he tells K. a story about "a man from the country who begs for admittance to the Law." The man from the country is told by the doorkeeper to the Law that he can't be admitted yet. He spends the rest of his life waiting for permission from the doorkeeper for admittance to the Law, and dies without attaining his goal.

In years of being in schools with teenagers I was often baffled and challenged by the workings of their maturing minds. But I learned early in my career that adolescents have an acute sense of fairness and quickly feel wronged when they believe they have been dealt with unjustly. I am still intrigued that Bill would choose ten days being grounded to epitomize his identity as a student and his four years at St. Francis as an irrational injustice of Kafkaesque proportions.

# 9

## THE NEW LUNAR SOCIETY

In February 1992, Gus, a junior, participated in a black-tie dinner sponsored by the New Lunar Society to mark the occasion of Charles Darwin's birthday. He described the dinner, embellishing certain details such as the presence of alcoholic beverages, in a letter to the editors of *The Quarterly Journal of the New Lunar Society*:

> The eight of us ate a marvelous meal, which included an almond soup, salmon, beef Wellington, and several different wines. At the opening of each bottle, we were given a verbose talk by Mr. Runge on the history and background of the wine. At the end of the meal, our host, Ms. Reigler, gave us a summary of Darwin and his theories. Lastly, Mr. Wheaton told us about Faraday and his electricity experiments. This was the finale of a wonderful evening.

Gus neglected to note that he used his own acting experience to play the role of a young, curious Charles Darwin while Mr. Runge played Charles' older brother Erasmus. The two impersonated siblings gleefully exploded hydrogen balloons to the surprise of the dinner guests.

The New Lunar Society was established in the spring of 1991 by Susan Reigler, Michael Runge, and John Wheaton, the three members of St. Francis High School's Science Department. The New Lunar Society was inspired by the eighteenth-century Lunar Society of Birmingham, England, two of whose founding members were Charles Darwin's grandfathers: Josiah Wedgwood and Erasmus Darwin. Inventor Benjamin Franklin was a corresponding member. The purpose of the St. Francis chapter was to encourage scientific activity among students, partly by establishing *The Quarterly Journal of the New Lunar Society*, which published articles by both students and teachers.

While St. Francis has had a number of noteworthy science teachers, the convergence of the diverse backgrounds, personalities, and interests of these three teachers created an unusually stimulating and fertile environment for the school's science students. Susan Reigler was a Louisville native, product of local public schools and the University of Louisville. She won a Humphrey Scholarship and was irrevocably changed by spending two years earning a graduate zoology degree, with one of her concentrations in entomology, at Oxford University. A consummate Anglophile and fervent proponent of Darwinian evolution, Susan was also a musician, a founding member of the Ars Femina chamber music ensemble, and restaurant critic for the Louisville *Courier-Journal*. Susan had a knack for devising offbeat projects for her biology students. One of my favorites was the yearly assignment to produce a creative writing piece describing a disease caused by a microorganism. I'll never forget tenth grader Janet Grayson's six-stanza song, "Malaria, Malaria," sung to the tune of "Que Sera, Sera." The third stanza goes:

When the sporozoa are little

The mosquito eats them. Then they

mature,

They lodge themselves in its midgut

Forming sporozites

Who swim in salivary glands.

Malaria. Damned Anopheles just had

to bite me,

Protozoa injected into me. I've got

malaria.

Ms. Reigler loved bugs, Darwin, coffee, music, good food, and cricket. She liked students as long as they applied rigor to self-discipline as well as their scientific endeavors. I remember a photo of Susan in the October 1985 issue of the student newspaper, wearing her white lab coat while holding a mug of coffee in one hand and Gregor, a teddy-bear-sized stuffed cockroach in the other. Susan was known by students as Miss Demeanor, because she surpassed all other teachers at turning in students for incidents of irresponsible behavior. Actually, Miss Demeanor's excessive zeal in handing out misdemeanors was a major factor in the school developing in 1986 a unique discipline system, the Discipline Review Board, that, with minor revisions, is still functioning well today, decades later.

Susan left St. Francis and high school teaching in the late 1990s to become a staff writer at the *Courier-Journal*, where she was primarily the restaurant critic, but also wrote science-related articles, thanks to her background. She was also a part-time university instructor, where her considerable knowledge, as well as her offbeat sense of humor, endeared her to many students.

When looking for new teachers, I sought candidates who were well qualified in terms of educational experience and degrees, possessed intellectual energy and curiosity, and had genuine interest and enthusiasm for the subjects they would teach. They also needed the self-confidence and flexibility to be in an intellectually rigorous, yet progressive, student-centered school. Over the years I learned that the teachers I sought would most likely come from other independent schools or from colleges and universities.

While I preferred candidates who had taught for at least three years, I occasionally hired a young, recent college graduate. In the summer of 1989, I had yet to hire a new math teacher, traditionally one of the hardest vacancies to fill. I received a phone call from Renu Lonial, a parent whose oldest son Sagar had graduated in 1985 and whose younger son was a current junior. She and her family had just returned from a trip to celebrate her son's graduation from Johns Hopkins. His roommate and close friend, Michael Runge, had joined them on the trip. Renu's son was entering medical school, but Michael had no plans yet for life after college. As they talked about what Michael might do, Renu's younger son Sayar said to him, "How about teaching? Maybe St. Francis could use you." Michael thought about it and asked Renu to check with me to see if there were any openings. She called and told me about Michael. He may have only been twenty-one, but his credentials were impressive— Presidential Scholar, Phi Beta Kappa, and a double major in biology and philosophy. As Renu described Michael, his brilliance was low key, submerged under an affable personality, which I confirmed during our telephone interview. He was clearly qualified to teach any high school math and science courses. Given Renu's and her son's strong recommendations and their familiarity with St. Francis, I felt confident in hiring Michael. He turned out to be a gifted teacher, able to explain virtually anything to students of all levels of ability in courses ranging from introductory chemistry to Advanced Placement calculus. With his keen intellect and natural teaching ability, he was unquestionably the most successful "rookie" I hired during my years at St. Francis.

Michael was red-green color-blind, not a problem for a math teacher, but problematic for someone teaching chemistry, as lab reactions are often detected by color changes. Any time there was a lab where the change in a reaction was from red to green or green to red, his students, being teenagers, chose not to tell him what was happening. But as he shared a supply closet with Susan Reigler, he could pop into her room through the closet. "Quick, what color is this?" She would give him the answer and he'd hurry back to class. Susan remembers a biology experiment in which she pulverized spinach with some alcohol and shone an LED flashlight through the test tube full of the mixture. The electrons in the chlorophyll jumped to another energy level and the tube glowed red instead of green. She and Michael were always exchanging nifty experiments, but when she rushed into his room to show him this one, of course, he was unimpressed. "What am I supposed to see here?" She had forgotten that to Michael it was just a tube of brown liquid.

John Wheaton's curly, wispy hair and beard gave him an Einsteinian flavor that only added to his effectiveness in teaching physics. I can see him now in his classroom with his hand on a Van de Graaff generator, his hair standing straight out in all directions, an electrified Afro. Like Susan and Michael, John was an unlikely individual to end up teaching at a small independent high school in Louisville, Kentucky. Originally from Long Island, he had gone to Princeton and majored in comparative literature. After graduation, he worked as a newspaper reporter for several years, his last stint being at the Owensboro *Messenger-Inquirer* in western Kentucky. John decided that life as a teacher might be more suitable for an unpretentious, soft-spoken Quaker and, having minored in physics in college, sought out the closest good physics masters degree program, which happened to be at the University of Louisville. While pursuing the degree, he was working in the education dean's office, where two or three of his coworkers had children at St. Francis. They recommended he ask if he could do his practice teaching at St. Francis, which he did, and I accepted. In March 1985, while John was there, the existing teacher told him that he and his wife were planning to leave, and suggested that John apply for the job. I was always looking for local teachers who might fit my requirements; John did. I offered him the job, he accepted, and taught at St. Francis for twenty-three years.

John had a remarkable ability to present complicated concepts clearly, in an accessible, stimulating manner. He exemplified for students an inquiring mind. Regularly attending conferences and summer institutes, he kept up with current developments in modern physics, especially particle physics and cosmology, and found ways to make their intriguing possibilities accessible to students. John's fascination with the concepts of physics was contagious and students who would never have thought of taking a physics course signed up for his classes. He developed three different physics courses for students with different levels of math/science ability and interest. John also created unusual half-year elective courses, including one called "The Science in Science Fiction," where students read science fiction classics and used the laws of physics to decide whether what happened in the books was scientifically possible. Unlike most high schools where a minority of students take physics, almost all of St. Francis students took at least one physics course. John's non-confrontative style was especially effective in encouraging young women to take physics and his classes typically had as many girls as boys. One of his female students, a graduate of M.I.T., named him her most influential high school teacher. And he was able to put his newspaper experience to good use as well, becoming adviser to the school paper.

Like Frank Cayce and me at St. Francis School in Goshen, none of these three teachers could have been hired by the local public-school system because they all lacked the required certification. But then, none of them would have applied for teaching positions in the public system due to the large classes and inability to design their own courses. One reason I founded an independent school was to be able to hire whomever I believed would be a good teacher and would flourish from having personal control over the courses they designed and taught. As with the original Lunar Society, the meeting of minds was a feast for the students.

# 10

## VINEGAR AND OIL

When St. Francis High School was scheduled to open for its first year in September, 1977, I needed eight full-time and four part-time teachers to teach sixty students spread across ninth, tenth and eleventh grades. The success of the new school depended on finding teachers whose backgrounds, personalities, and skills would provide a quality of instruction superior to that available at local public and parochial high schools. I posted notices at nearby colleges and universities and placed classified ads, but, given the limitations of the local pool of teachers, I also embarked on a national search. Using placement agencies specializing in independent school teachers, I reviewed applications, selected the most promising candidates, and brought them to Louisville for personal interviews. One applicant came in from Indianapolis for his interview. He later described it this way:

The interview was conducted at the Cathedral over on

Second Street ... After the interview we piled into Tom Pike's Volkswagen van for a tour of Louisville and came by the school building ... It was just this huge, crazy, dirty, open, messy, old, wide third floor ... As Pike toured me through this sort of falling down wreck, he points out where the Science Labs are going to be here and the Art Studio is going to be here and here we are going to have this big meeting room, and on and on. It was really amazing to see a guy with a new idea for a brand-new thing that really had not any concrete substance yet, but was committed to it. So it was a good interview, I thought. We had a lovely time. ... the more I thought about the possibilities, the more interesting it sounded ... and I decided, you know, why not? I was thirty at the time. A great opportunity for me, being on the ground floor of something.

I also remembered that interview with Neil McCullough. When I had begun recruiting teachers, the school's facilities were just beginning to be constructed, and I literally had nothing but words to convey what the new school would be like, physically and philosophically.

By the end of the afternoon, I had decided to offer Neil the full-time English position. He had strong recommendations from supervisors and colleagues at his current school. Full of energy, well-educated, with good experience, he was obviously committed to teaching English and enthusiastic about the prospect of being part of a new school. Neil's slicked back hair, bushy mustache, and articulate but quirky speech patterns hinted at an offbeat personality which would appeal to teenagers.

Anyone who thinks that teaching is easy has never been a teacher or observed good teachers at work. There are few tasks as demanding and complex as successfully engaging a group of students in a series of learning activities over a class period. Imagine repeating this feat five or six times a day over a hundred-and-seventy-five-day school year. Think of conducting an orchestra when the musicians have different skill levels, are on different pages of the score, with the score being rewritten as the musicians play, and yet maintaining an underlying, coherent theme that is heard by everyone. Then, add to that challenge St. Francis' progressive, personalized approach which encourages individual expression and independent thinking.

One of the school's most memorable and controversial instructors, Neil McCullough was a masterful English teacher, his fascination with literature and grammar transmitted with intensity and humor. Neil expected and insisted that his students learn. He was loud, brusque, and sarcastic. He had little patience for slackers and sloppy work but would spend as much time as needed to help hardworking marginal students succeed.

Students at St. Francis participated in the annual evaluation of teachers; as always their comments about Neil conveyed a sense of his style:

"Mr. McCullough has somewhat of a short fuse."

"... a great teacher and a very eccentric man who loves English and loves to teach."

"It would be impossible not to learn from McCullough."

But there were always a few students intimidated by his impatient, strong, in-your-face approach. Neil's very identity as teacher and person seemed to depend upon every student responding positively to his efforts. And, when they didn't, his frustration was sometimes expressed inappropriately. Several times a year, there were complaints about his behavior. Typically the "short fuse" sparked his yelling at a student or colleague with sarcastic or foul language. When we met to discuss incidents, he was always remorseful, as he especially regretted upsetting students. The two of us would meet with the student and he would sincerely apologize.

Periodically I wrestled with Neil's being an outstanding teacher for most of his students, but seriously problematic for a few of them. I told myself that surely they would experience difficult teachers in college, that surviving Neil's mercurial personality and high academic expectations would be good preparation. I also reminded myself that his students experienced at least four other teachers during a school day, all of whom would have different styles than he. Neil taught at St. Francis for twenty-five years.

It was a Thursday afternoon in early April 1995 and I had flown into Washington DC to find a new teacher for an expanding history program. I planned to interview candidates Friday and Saturday at the Independent Educational Services (IES) recruitment fair at the Dupont Circle Hotel, a small, comfortable hotel in one of my favorite DC neighborhoods. IES specialized in providing teacher and administrator candidates to the thousand plus independent schools in the US and was one of the resources I regularly used to hire new teachers. While it was late in the hiring season, I had yet to find a history teacher who suited me. This was IES's last job fair for the hiring season, so I had no choice but to attend.

Christy Bowman was about my height, five-eight, medium build, straight blond hair in a practical, out of eyes cut. Her face, voice, and general manner expressed confidence, competence, friendliness, and a maturity beyond her twenty-five years. I knew from her file that Christy had grown up in Chapel Hill, North Carolina; her father was a researcher and teacher at the Duke University Medical Center. After studying U.S. History and African Studies at Earlham College, she had gone to the University of Oregon and earned a Masters degree in U.S. History, focusing on women's history. She currently taught history at Princeton Day School, replacing a teacher who was on leave for a year.

Christy and I walked to the St. Francis table in the interviewing room and, as I began to sit down, I realized that my back would not survive a half an hour's sitting.

"This is a bit unusual, but my back is really bothering me and I'm not going to be able to sit for half an hour. The sun is shining; it's nice outside. Do you mind going for a walk with me and talking as we walk?"

We got our jackets and spent the next forty-five minutes walking around the residential neighborhoods north of Dupont Circle.

"Tell me about your year in Princeton. I remember Princeton Day as a pretty high-powered school."

"It sure is. Most of the parents are academics or executives with high expectations. This is my first experience teaching and it's exhausting and challenging, but I love the kids and love teaching history. I thought this was what I wanted to do, but now I know for sure." Her voice was animated and sincere.

"What has been hardest for you during your first year of teaching?"

"I bring a lot of energy and enthusiasm to my classes and I don't seem to have many discipline problems. What I struggle with the most is being able to engage each of my students at a level that challenges, but doesn't overwhelm them. I had assumed that this would be easy with small classes, but it really isn't. Each student is such a different mix of ability and personality. Some seem to learn best from my lectures, while others do better with discussions or working in small groups. It's been hard to find enough time to prepare my classes as thoroughly as I want to."

Christy had done her homework and was familiar with the philosophy, curriculum, and programs at St. Francis. She wanted to know all about my starting the school and how it had changed during its nineteen years. I talked at some length about the evolution of the school's curriculum and the participation of teachers in decision-making. She was excited about history teachers being able to teach semester electives in addition to the core history curriculum. "I would love to offer an African Studies or Women's Studies elective, or focus for a semester on the Civil War."

The more we talked, the more Christy seemed a good match for St. Francis. Forty-five minutes walking and talking went by quickly, and, when we got back to the hotel, I told her I would call her after I returned to school and sorted out my interviews. She responded enthusiastically that she had enjoyed our conversation and was definitely interested in the job.

My subsequent interviews went well, but none of them matched the immediate connection and pleasure of my time with Christy. She was clearly the first choice for the position, but I did have two backup candidates in case she didn't work out. She visited St. Francis, liked the school, and seemed comfortable with teachers and students. I checked the next morning with Jim and Tim, who would be her history colleagues and who had met with her during the visit. They concurred with my decision to offer her the job.

Christy accepted my offer and taught at St. Francis for thirteen years. She was one of the school's most respected and loved teachers when she moved back to North Carolina in 2008 to work in a school near where her parents lived. Christy had many strengths as a teacher, especially her knowledge and love of U.S. History, African Studies, and Women's Studies and her consummate preparation and organization. But essential to her effectiveness were a secure sense of who she was and the respect she had for each of her students as maturing young adults. They felt valued by her, even when they screwed up, goofed off, or loafed. She would gently, firmly insist they shape up, and would help them do it. Patient and unflappable, she was centered in a way that made her both accessible to students and immune to manipulation.

Over the years I developed a list of characteristics for effective

St. Francis High School teachers. Most necessary were a strong sense of personal identity, a passion for the subject being taught, a command of one's subject, a willingness to insist that students learn, and respect and affection for teenagers. Important, but less critical were modeling being a good learner, collegiality, and involvement with students outside of the classroom. Christy possessed all of these traits in varying degrees: an unusually balanced, highly competent teacher of history. But teachers less well-balanced and possessing fewer of these traits, could in their own idiosyncratic way be highly effective, albeit with a smaller percentage of their students. Christy Bowman and Neil McCullough were as different in personality as any two teachers I ever hired. While he lacked her patience, centeredness, and self-confidence, his passion and high energy infused an encyclopedic knowledge of English. When I meet St. Francis alumni, I often ask them to tell me the teachers from whom they learned the most. Neil's name is almost always on their list, Christy's almost as often.

# 11

## RECOVERY

As I hung up the phone, I decided to walk over to University Hospital, just a couple of blocks from St. Francis, to see if I could be of help to Cathy's father and her brother, Austin, an eighth grader. I learned that she was just coming out of surgery and would be unable to have visitors for several days. But they told me that a group of Cathy and Samantha's friends were in a waiting room adjacent to the operating rooms. Feeling both concern and curiosity I decided to join them.

Going down the hall, I heard a chorus of adolescent voices, a mix of frenetic, anxious sounds coupled with the hum of quiet conversations. I walked into a room crowded with teenagers, the energy of their presence and the power of their emotions overwhelming the sterile, generic hospital waiting room. Some sat in chairs and on a couch, others in small groups on the carpeted floor. My administrator's boundaries were immediately breached as palpable grief cut through to the love of teenagers, which had led me to discover my calling as an educator. My eyes began to fill with tears and I paused for a moment to regain my composure.

It was Winter Break and I had been in my office that Monday morning, enjoying an empty, quiet school and looking forward to a relaxed week. The phone had rung and it was Cathy Lewis' father, George, calling about the accident. Ignoring friends' warnings not to drink and drive, Cathy and her best friend Samantha had climbed into Cathy's car Sunday night, sped east on Ky. 22, and crashed head-on into a tree. Samantha, a junior at Seneca, died at the scene and Cathy was seriously injured. Police said that they believed alcohol had been a factor in the crash.

Alcohol use is a fairly constant backdrop in adolescent life. But unlike other substances illegal or forbidden to teenagers, which impinged on the daily routine because of a student occasionally caught dealing on or around the school, underaged drinking was something that occurred away from campus and outside of the school day. Certainly, I and members of the faculty would overhear kids talking about drinking at a party outside school. And there were sometimes issues on school trips over Spring Break: on a cross-country ski excursion in Michigan, some students (including my own son) had been caught drinking in the hotel lobby; on a Florida trip there had been nocturnal student drinking on the beach. But Cathy's accident was one of the rare instances when the consequences of alcohol use had public and tragic consequences for the entire school.

George was at University Hospital, where Cathy was undergoing surgery. Exhausted and upset, he explained that Cathy was in the Intensive Care Unit in critical condition. Amanda, Cathy's mother, was on her way home from Colorado where she had been skiing with friends and was due back in a couple of hours. One of them would call me when they got the surgeon's report.

A bright, outgoing, energetic teenager, Cathy was tall, lean, with bobbed, straight, brown hair. Her parents had divorced when she was a child. She lived with her mother but spent two days each week with her father. A transfer student, at St. Francis for only a semester, she had adjusted easily to her new school and was doing better academically than at her previous, public school, Seneca High. Currently maintaining a 'B' average in St. Francis' more demanding courses, Cathy enjoyed the small classes and was an enthusiastic participant in class discussions. While comfortable with her peers at St. Francis, her active social life revolved mainly around her Seneca friends, especially Samantha. There had been rumors about Cathy's drinking, but we had seen no evidence at school of a problem with alcohol use.

As I stood in the doorway of the waiting room, I recognized three St. Francis students, but did not know most of the kids, whom I assumed were Seneca students.

I went over to the St. Francis students, told them I knew Cathy's parents appreciated their coming, and sat down with them. Only Betsy had been at the party and she was describing to Joan and Marian how two friends had pleaded with Cathy and Samantha not to leave in their car. Betsy pointed to the friends, who were particularly distressed because, looking for Samantha and Cathy, they had come across the accident scene. They had watched workers from three volunteer fire departments take ninety minutes to cut the girls out of the wreckage.

I sat with the St. Francis students, mostly listening as they and other girls around us relived the events of the evening. Talking, crying, hugging, they consoled each other in grief for Samantha and concern for Cathy's critical condition. The atmosphere was charged with emotion as they dealt with the shattering of the adolescent illusion of invulnerability: "But it won't happen to me." They all realized that it could have been any of them last night in the front seats of the black Ford Escort. With the typical frankness and compassion of adolescence, they alternated between anger—"Why

99

the hell did she drive drunk?"—and concern for Cathy and all that faced her in a future irrevocably changed.

Amanda called me that afternoon to say that Cathy was doing better and was expected to fully recover physically. Amanda thought it would be five or six weeks before she would be back in school. Her badly broken legs were expected to heal, but it would be several months before she could walk normally. Steel rods had been inserted in her femurs. She would have intensive physical therapy until she was stable on crutches.

Cathy, in and out of consciousness in the ICU because of surgery and medication, was not told about Samantha until her mother arrived. Cathy later told me that of the two weeks in the hospital, she remembered "only small bursts of feelings between the four or five surgeries. Once I was told about Samantha, my friends kept me going, they were all awesome."

I told Amanda not to worry about school. The thought never entered my mind not to have Cathy return to St. Francis. We would provide her with assignments whenever she was ready to do school work and help her get caught up. Amanda was especially concerned about Cathy's emotional well-being. Together at Seneca for two years until Cathy transferred to St. Francis for her junior year, she and Samantha had remained close, often spending evenings and weekends together. How would Cathy deal with being responsible for the death of her best friend? How was she going to be able to face her and Samantha's friends, Samantha's parents, and her classmates and teachers at St. Francis?

Talking to me later, Cathy remembered that she "actually never had a lot of trouble facing anyone other than Samantha's family; that always tore me up. But they were very understanding. They knew that either of us could have been driving that night." Cathy told me about receiving support from people who had similar experiences. "I had lots of visitors—friends, family, people I babysat for, and people I didn't even know. I got cards and flowers from people that I had met throughout my life, including old teachers from grade school. I had tons of support."

Once she was mobile, Cathy went to court. The local MADD chapter pushed the District Attorney to try her as an adult and put her in jail. Being a minor with a good school record and having a skilled attorney, she was placed on probation, but required to attend AA meetings and do extensive community service. When Cathy returned to school, the sight of her on crutches was a daily reminder to her classmates of the risks of drinking and driving. During the next six months, Cathy did a number of programs at schools throughout the Louisville area, openly talking about her alcohol use and the accident. I remember well the one she did in October as a senior at St. Francis, when she spoke to the faculty and student body. Candidly, poignantly, she told her story of drinking too much when partying on weekends. The theatre was eerily quiet and she had the rapt attention of her audience of students and teachers. She told about the night in February when she and Samantha ignored their friends, got in their car and left the party. She described how driving drunk she lost control, ran into a tree, and killed her best friend. Her stark, straightforward witness to what happened was the most effective program on teenage drinking that I ever attended.

Cathy successfully finished her junior year and graduated the following June. She attended Vanderbilt University and, after graduation, chose to stay in Nashville. Always interested in art, she currently does development work for an art gallery. She has maintained contact with Samantha's mother, now divorced and living in California. The last time I spoke with Cathy, she seemed settled and comfortable with her life in Nashville.

# 12

## DISCOMFORT

"Angela, George, come on in. Have a seat." I gestured to the cluster of three chairs in my office. They were girlfriend and boyfriend, both juniors—Angela petite, confident, contained, long dark hair, George also short, a scrappy soccer player, baseball cap on backwards.

I had been out of town and when I got back, Tim Marshall had told me about concerns he had with Charles Green, the French teacher. "Tim mentioned an incident that happened as you were leaving for lunch," I began. "Tell me about it."

George spoke first. "We were walking out the front door when Charles made an obscene gesture at us with his hand. We were surprised and just kept on walking. I felt weird about it and it made Angela uncomfortable."

"No other teacher has ever done that," Angela added, "and I wondered what was going on with Mr. Green."

"You know," George continued, "he flirts a lot with all the girls."

I looked back at Angela. "George also told Tim that there were other times that Charles did similar things. Evidently no one wanted to report them, partly because Charles is on the school's harassment committee. Tell me what you know about any other incidents."

"Last October, he asked what I was doing for Halloween. I told him that maybe I'll go trick or treating. He then asked me if I was a little old for that. I told him no, I think I can pass for twelve. He looked me up and down and said there's no way you can pass for twelve. It surprised me and I felt a bit uncomfortable. It's true what George said. Charles does flirt with the girls, especially Erin and Kim."

"Are you uncomfortable now in French class?"

"Not really, but it's my least favorite class."

"Does what has happened have anything to do with that?"

"Maybe."

I thanked Angela for her willingness to talk to me and complimented George for taking their concerns to the Dean of Students. I told them that Charles's behavior was totally unacceptable. I said that over the next few days I would quietly ask around for additional information, and would then meet with Charles. Angela agreed to talk with me again at the end of the week.

In the late 1980s and early 1990s, there had been a significant increase in reporting of harassment incidents in schools. Federal laws were passed prohibiting sexual harassment among students, among employees, and between students and school employees. Schools were advised to establish formal policies to cover all kinds of harassment. In the spring of 1994, a year before this incident, a St. Francis faculty-staff committee led by school counselor Janey Butler had developed a formal harassment policy, which covered behavior of both students and employees. Charles Green was one of the faculty members who served on the committee. Formally adopted by the staff later that spring, St. Francis' new policy had gone into effect at the beginning of the 1994-1995 school year. I am certain that since I retired, this policy has been updated, likely more than once, to keep up with changing laws and understanding about sexual harassment.

Charles had begun teaching at St. Francis mid-year, replacing a new teacher who resigned because of unsatisfactory performance. He had been recommended by a former parent, who was chair of the modern languages department at the University of Louisville. Charles was the best candidate from a meager list of applicants. A Baptist minister in his late thirties, he had been a music educator and spent a number of years training choirs. While he hadn't taught classroom French before, Charles was bilingual and had lots of experience working with teenagers. I wrote in my interview notes that he "was enthusiastic, clearly liked kids, and seemed to have a good sense of himself." He had appeared to be a solid prospect, who with supervision could turn out to be a successful career teacher.

A couple of days after the incident with Angela, mathematics teacher Jan Leland came to me with additional concerns, which she had heard from several of her female students. They felt he was not a good teacher—disorganized, poorly prepared—and they were "learning nothing." One student, Mary, also told Jan that Charles stared at them and stood too close to them. Mary also remembered a discussion in class about abortion when he ignored the boys and talked only to the girls, which also bothered them.

That afternoon I met again with Angela. Tim Marshall sat in with us.

"How's it been going in French class?"

"I don't know what to do, Mr. Pike. Every day it gets worse and it's a struggle to go to class. I was uneasy about what he said about Halloween and I shrugged it off. But, because of what happened with George and me, I feel uncomfortable. I try to just do my work, but I can't."

"What do you want to do?"

"Last night at dinner I told my stepfather about Mr. Green making me uneasy. He said he was going to call you. He suggested that I move out of the class."

"That's what Mr. Marshall and I want you to do. You can finish the French course independently with Ms. Bernard and join Ms. Hammond's photography class. I know you wanted to take photography, but couldn't because it conflicted with French."

Angela relaxed and smiled, "Oh thank you, Mr. Pike, I would like that."

Her stepfather called me the next day. We knew each other fairly well, as his daughter, Elizabeth, Angela's stepsister, had graduated from St. Francis the previous June. He was satisfied with the plan for Angela, but wanted to be sure that the independent study program had adequate oversight. He wanted me to meet with Charles, but was not filing a formal complaint. I explained that I was still investigating Charles's behavior and would call back in a couple of days to let him know what I planned to do.

I then met with Janey, who would join me in talking with Charles. While I tended to be analytical and abstract, Janey was concrete and concise. Her ability to help less able students organize their thoughts, materials, and lives was of equal help to me when I needed to pare my words and actions. She was also one of the two staff members elected to serve as mediators for harassment complaints brought under the school's new policy.

Janey was aware of issues with Charles's teaching performance. Some of the students she worked with had complained about his casual approach to teaching. Issues of organization and preparation had also come up on his annual evaluations. Janey had not heard about his making some of the female students uncomfortable, and she was surprised and concerned.

"Whether Charles's actions are intentional or not, we have a serious problem. Our intervention should include this incident as part of a broader set of concerns that he be more professional and cautious: he causes students to feel uneasy. I think this will be more productive than if we just accuse him of sexual harassment."

That made sense to me. I had observed Charles's teaching twice over the year he had been at St. Francis and in our post-observation meetings addressed specific concerns regarding his teaching. He had done well enough his first semester at St. Francis that I gave him a contract for the following school year. I did note in my journal that he "is not putting in the time he needs to plan his courses—it's more than just being laid back. I need to hold him accountable." A couple of days later, "I met with Charles—I think he will put in more time; he's enjoying the work and the kids." This was a typical example of my perennial optimism, usually a helpful trait working with teenagers, but often risky with teachers.

I told Janey I would revisit those issues and then move to the recent incident with Angela and George and the Halloween incident with Angela. As founding Head of St. Francis High School and in charge of all aspects of the school for seventeen years, I had dealt with financial crises, personnel problems, several student suicides and fatal car accidents, and occasional student suspensions and dismissals. I had grown into my calling as a progressive educator and felt confident in my ability to be decisive, fair, unflappable, and compassionate, even in confronting potentially explosive situations.

Janey and I met with Charles after school the following Monday. He was dressed in jeans, a polo shirt, and dirty sneakers, looking more like a student than a teacher. St. Francis has no dress code for faculty or students other than appropriateness for a progressive school environment, comfortable and respectful. Charles was one of three bearded, long-haired teachers, his attire typically casual, bordering on sloppy.

"I've visited several of your classes over the two semesters you've taught at St. Francis. We've met twice to discuss my observations and your student evaluations and I've told you that your organization, preparation, and class management needed improvement. I have expressed concerns about an overly relaxed approach in both teaching style and in interactions with students. I recently learned of things you have done that made some students feel uncomfortable. There are two incidents that truly concern me."

I described the questionable interaction with George and Angela and the incident with Angela last Halloween. I told him that the Halloween interaction was an example of what several girls meant when they said that Charles flirted with them. "It's the way he looks at us, stands too close to us."

Charles's response was immediate, one of surprise and defensiveness, and he jumped up.

"This really blows me away. I did not make a finger gesture at George and Angela. That's not in my vocabulary. It's their word against mine. I do remember the Halloween incident with Angela. I was just kidding with her."

Charles was angry, bewildered, and hurt by my accusations of impropriety. He complained about St. Francis students' "aberrant sexual values" and their lack of "spiritual values." He wished that the school did more to "expose students to religious values." I told him he needed to think about our concerns and the incidents in question. We set a time to meet again the next day.

After he and Janey left, I relaxed and thought for several minutes. Charles seemed totally unaware that his words and actions had a sexual component. His comment about sexual values had a disturbing tone. It made me wonder whether, as a conservative Christian minister, he was comfortable with his own sexuality and his church's teachings on sexuality.

The next day Janey and I talked for a couple of minutes before Charles was due to meet with us. What concerned her most about Charles's reaction was his lack of awareness and clarity and the defensive complaint about the poor values of students and parents.

We decided that we must be clear and succinct about what he needed to do differently.

Charles came in a couple of minutes later, subdued and anxious. He wore a shirt with a collar, khakis, not jeans, and he had trimmed his hair and beard.

"I've thought a lot about what you said yesterday and my wife and I talked at length last night. I've been doing youth work for a decade. I enjoy being with teenagers, girls and boys, teaching them, singing with them, playing pickup basketball games. I feel at ease with them. I'm affectionate and physical by nature. It upsets me to think that some of them aren't comfortable with me. Obviously, I must be more careful."

Janey responded. "The more personalized nature of St. Francis can be difficult for teachers. Having small classes and knowing students well can enhance learning, but being too familiar has its risks, as you've discovered. You might observe Tim Marshall and Abby Bernard as models. They have friendly, personal relationships with lots of students. But, they make clear through their demeanor, organization, and expectations that they are the adults, responsible for learning taking place in their classes."

I added, "You'll be relieved that Angela's stepfather is not making a formal complaint under the school's Harassment Policy, but he does want action taken. Angela has been withdrawn from your class. She'll complete her French credit doing independent study with Ms. Bernard. Do not try to apologize to Angela; she just wants out of your class. You must be more professional in your relationships with students and in preparing and teaching your classes. There can be no further incidents of physical closeness and excessive familiarity. Another such incident will be viewed formally as harassment, with the possible result of dismissal."

"I understand, Tom. You don't have to worry about me."

There were no more incidents. Charles was able to behave

appropriately in his interactions with students, but unable to become more organized and better prepared for classes. Not willing to spend the necessary time and effort to become more than just a barely competent teacher, his performance failed to meet St. Francis' expectations. Charles's contract was not renewed and a new French teacher was hired the following year.

# 13

## BOUNDARIES

According to the Association of American Colleges Peer Harassment pamphlet, sexual harassment is … persistent sexual attention, especially when it continues after a clear indication of nonreciprocity of feelings.

First-period classes had just begun and sophomore Emily Hall had settled in a corner of the Commons Room to read the morning newspaper. She was nearing her last day at St. Francis before moving to Ohio where her mother had taken a teaching job at a small liberal arts college.

"Emily." She looked up to see Mr. Williams, her history teacher.

"I need to talk with you. Can we go to the Quiet Study Area?"

"Sure, Mr. Williams. I don't have a class and my homework's all done."

She followed him out of the Commons Room and down the hall. As they went around the corner there was David Maddox, a classmate, waiting for them. Tall, shy, and awkward, physical coordination had yet to catch up with his lanky frame. Hidden behind large glasses which framed a pleasant, earnest face was the most computer-savvy mind at St. Francis. I was unaware at the time that David also was known for the unnerving habit of staring at female classmates and then giving them gum afterwards.

"David likes you, Emily," Mr. Williams began, "and wants to say goodbye. He asked me to set up a meeting with you."

Mr. Williams walked away, leaving her with an uncomfortable, inarticulate David and several moments of awkward silence.

"I don't care if you have a crush on me. I've informed you on several occasions that I'm not interested. Leave me alone." She turned and walked off before he could say anything. Or at least this is what I have in my notes. According to Emily much later, she was too shocked by the whole situation to do more than mumble something inconsequential and quickly retreat. It took a few days of reflection, she says, to figure out what was going on and how messed up it felt to her.

She eventually sought out Mr. Williams in his classroom during a free period to confront him about what had happened that morning.

"I'm appalled that you, a teacher, would put me in such an awkward position. I have made it clear to David that I do not want to be friends and told him to stop paying attention to me."

"I'm sorry you feel that way, Emily. I was just trying to help a lonely, bashful student and didn't think it would be a big deal."

"Mr. Williams, you don't get it. David's attentions are unwanted and make me uncomfortable. If I weren't leaving, I would file a harassment complaint against both of you."

She spun around and walked out of the classroom.

Emily moved to Ohio with her mother and completed tenth grade at the local public high school. While a well-regarded school, it was six times as big as St. Francis High School. Not feeling challenged and stimulated by her courses and teachers, she decided to move back to Louisville to live with her father and spend her junior and senior years at St. Francis. Emily was unusually mature and confident for her age, so I was not surprised by this decision.

Two months into Emily's junior year, St. Francis' counselor, Janey Butler, came up to me after Morning Meeting and told me that a letter from Emily Hall was in my mailbox. She and Emily wanted to meet with me and we set a time for later that day. (Here, too, Emily's memory differs from my notes: "I remember a very uncomfortable meeting in which I was the only woman present. It would have been great to have a female counselor through all this.") On the way back to my office, I went by the faculty room and picked up Emily's letter. Two-pages long, typed, single-spaced, it was addressed to Gary Williams, her history teacher, with copies to Tim Marshall, Dean of Students, and me.

Dear Mr. Williams,

Recent events concerning your continued intervention between David Maddox and me have escalated to the point where I can no longer remain silent. You have done things that have been inappropriate and made me feel uncomfortable. You have encouraged sexual harassment of one student toward another and I wish it to stop. …

Emily's parents were divorced; her older brother and sister had also attended St. Francis High School. I considered her the most outgoing and assertive of the Hall siblings, all of them excellent students.

Her letter went on to list the events which led to her accusations, starting with a detailed description of the incident with David and Mr. Williams the previous October, a year earlier, when she was a tenth grader.

Emily's letter continued:

… Since returning to St. Francis, I have on repeated occasions rejected David's frequent attempts at interesting me or being friendly when it felt stifling and invasive of my privacy. He has held open doors for me when they were already open, he has made most people in our grade aware of his interest in me, and he has constantly reminded me that he wanted to establish a relationship. David's behavior and Mr. Williams's encouragement constitute sexual harassment, even though I believe it was not their intent to make me uncomfortable. Nevertheless, these were unwanted advances encouraged by a figure of authority. .

When I finished reading Emily's letter, I marveled at the skill and confidence with which it was crafted. But its portrayal of Gary Williams's poor judgment in supporting a lonesome male student disturbed me. In small schools like St. Francis, teachers and students become well acquainted with each other. Such informal relationships provide important opportunities for support and encouragement and help motivate students to be successful. But balancing friendship with professionalism can be tricky, as Gary had discovered. And while some students benefited from that closeness, others could perceive it as improper favoritism.

When I met later that day with Emily and Janey, they had already planned what was needed to bring closure to the situation. In her letter to Mr. Williams, Emily instructed him to share the letter with David and also tell him that she had given copies of the letter to me and Tim Marshall.

"Mr Pike, since Mr. Williams has been the go-between for David's feelings in the past, it's fitting that he relay this absolutely final message. I want him to speak directly to David in the Dean of

Students' office, with Mr. Marshall as witness."

"Emily, I'm really impressed with your letter and the way you have handled this situation."

"And, Mr. Pike. I still need you to meet with Mr. Williams about what has happened. If there are no further problems, I won't file an official complaint under the school's Harassment Policy. I want you to put a copy of my letter in both David's and Mr. Williams's school files. I don't need to meet with Gary Williams, I only want him to be my history teacher."

While I never knew exactly how Gary Williams or David Maddox responded to Emily's letter, there were no further incidents of unwanted attention reported to me. The three apparently regained comfort in necessary school contact. As Emily wrote in her letter to Gary, "Please understand that if this behavior is significantly altered, I see no obstacle against reconciliation between us." I don't know how an incident like this would play out today, or how I would deal with it differently; what I can say is that Emily's letter was well-stated by the one mature individual involved.

I discovered much later that Emily's memory of this incident differs radically from my own. "More often in these situations," she wrote me when I asked her about it, "the women are initially paralyzed, not immediately articulate in sticking up for themselves. All of this talk about Emily as articulate fails to convey that it undermined her confidence walking the halls, and the involvement of a teacher made her feel gaslit and crazy for objecting because a teacher was involved so it must be okay, right? Call it harassment, please," she continued. "Just for what it's worth, I would personally characterize it as an early lesson in what harassment looks like when it doesn't actually involve non-consensual touch, and how that, paired with the express endorsement of an authority figure, can be just as uncomfortable for a student." My memory of this incident was very likely affected by my equal sympathy for all parties involved, and very likely to Emily's detriment. While I may have been wrong about how Emily felt about her handling of it as an adolescent, her clear-eyed analysis of the situation looking back tells me that I wasn't so far off in my sense of the person she would become, despite the mistakes made by everyone else involved.

# 14

## A CHICK COURSE

Checking my mailbox one morning, I found a five-page essay entitled "A Chick Course," written by Bruce, a shy, brilliant senior. A key member of the school's top-ranked Quick Recall team, Bruce was known for his skill in answering math and science questions. "A Chick Course" was a long, detailed protest about his Modern World course on social movements of the twentieth century—labor, civil, and women's rights. Bruce complained that the teacher, Christy Bowman, discriminated against him, because "All discussion and class activity is centered around techniques specifically designed to benefit girls." He recognized these techniques from articles and essays that Ms. Bowman had assigned the class. He claimed that, like most boys with "linear, binary minds," he learned best "by reading, lectures, and working alone." He concluded, "I am deeply offended by a course that seems to favor girls in the class by defeating my natural intelligence."

Gender bias should have been an unlikely issue to become a

major controversy at St. Francis High School. Since its inception in 1977, the school has prided itself on challenging and affirming its students, female and male. The school's small size of a hundred and thirty students and student-teacher ratio of 8:1 were deliberate choices made for the sake of personalizing instruction. While certainly aware of gender differences—social, biological, emotional, and intellectual—we observed as much variation in learning styles among boys and among girls as between boys and girls.

When I read Bruce's "A Chick Course" essay, I was at first amused and then struck with a sense of irony. I found it hard to feel sorry for Bruce and viewed the incident as an important learning experience for him. I asked him to meet with me in my office. He arrived, clearly uncomfortable, but anxious to plead his case.

"Bruce, I've read your thoughtfully written essay. While I understand your frustration, I don't see a serious problem. Modern World seems to be the only one of your five classes where the teacher's approach favors girls' learning styles. Am I right in assuming that you have no problems in AP Calculus and AP Chemistry, your Spanish class, or with loud, argumentative Mr. McCullough in English IV?"

"Yes, the problem is only in Ms. Bowman's class," his tone implying that my point was irrelevant to him.

"So maybe now you can better understand what some young women feel when asked to do a step-by-step mathematical proof when they would prefer to examine how language and imagery are used in a novel." I would not likely use this comparison today.

"But I would get a better grade if I could learn my way,"

I told him that even if he got a 'B' it wouldn't affect college admissions. "You've already been accepted by Rice, your first choice."

Bruce was not happy, but grudgingly accepted my unwillingness to transfer him to another class or to interfere with Ms. Bowman's teaching style. I sensed that he just wanted to be heard and didn't really expect any changes. Bruce survived Modern World with a 'B' and graduated with honors.

At the time, the incident seemed to be an isolated situation with an atypical male teenager. But I had completely forgotten a staff meeting discussion the previous May, eight months before Bruce's lament. For the first time in the school's history, all of the elected class representatives to the School Committee for the coming year were girls. The minutes from the May 1995 staff meeting reported a lively discussion about whether the school had a problem affirming its male students.

Possible sources of such a problem were suggested:

Types of students drawn to St. Francis; i.e., more assertive females, less aggressive, less competitive males;

Lack of strong male role models at home;

Gender developmental differences;

Girls' behavior being praised more often than boys';

Guys letting girls do all the work.

While someone voiced a need to find ways to "build up" boys, no specific strategies were proposed. Weary from nine months of working with teenagers, we had left for vacation. The concerns we had expressed somehow disappeared over the summer. They remained dormant throughout the next school year, 1995-1996, except for my meeting with Bruce.

The following school year, in February 1997, a "Manifesto," written and signed by two senior boys, was posted on the walls of the main hallway of the school.

> In our earnestness to combat the problem of sexism, we have blinded ourselves to the reality: there is no discrimination against girls at St. Francis High School. The teachers' attitudes, but more importantly those of the students themselves, ironically succeed in creating the very problem they hope to eradicate. Males and females have always enjoyed equal attention and encouragement at St. Francis; attempts to augment the girls' side (which is thought to be neglected) shortchange the boys. The entire school suffers from this well-intended, but poorly administered effort to keep the scales balanced. Even more troubling … are the attitudes of the students themselves, who create a social climate where the masculine is under attack, something to be stamped out. The males themselves are the most guilty, for they have retreated into the roles of goofy, charming fools whose primary responsibility is to make the girls laugh. … We have forced our female classmates to shoulder the load themselves. Because their views are the only ones considered with any seriousness in class, the discussions and consensus reached in class tend to disregard and even discredit males and what they have done. … We have been intellectually henpecked.

Carl was a high achieving scholar-athlete, with pale complexion and curly, reddish hair. Sean's long, dark hair covered an inquiring, creative brain, which he applied to what interested him: music, literature, and film. In the several pages of the "Manifesto," Sean and Carl criticized their classmates, especially other males, as well as the adults in the school for their failure to adequately affirm the school's male students. They described the domination of class discussions by girls and the favoring of female students by both male and female teachers. Carl and Sean argued that academic excellence was far more acceptable and encouraged among females.

Several weeks later, Mike, a ninth grader, posted an "anti-Manifesto."

> Neither of the "Manifesto" authors are freshmen. ... They have no idea if freshman males make insightful comments in class or if they joke around all the time ... Simply because we joke around in the halls doesn't mean we cannot pull it together inside the classroom. It is possible to have fun and make good grades as well. Balance between humor and seriousness is what keeps us sane.

Subsequent discussions among faculty members and older students confirmed a healthier climate in the ninth- and tenth-grade classes. They also supported Sean and Carl's well-documented allegations regarding problems in Junior and Senior courses. Had the school's well-intended efforts to ensure that girls not be short-changed somehow gone awry?

The main agenda item at the next staff meeting was discussion of the two Manifestos and what they exposed regarding gender bias at St. Francis. Staff meetings included both teachers and administrative staff, around thirty people, roughly equal numbers of women and men. The diversity of their backgrounds and personalities guaranteed lively meetings.

The notes from the March 1997 meeting are still enlightening today, as issues of gender and learning continue to be relevant at all schools, not just St. Francis. Our discussion encompassed a number of points, among them:

> During the school's twenty-year history, times of male dominance have cycled with those of female.

A generally weak sports program and poor computer and science facilities were obstacles in attracting male students.

Strong female students who felt neglected at large coed public schools often transferred to St. Francis as did intellectual, nonathletic boys.

Students and their parents lacked a sense of what being masculine means in the late-twentieth century.

The school's generally "soft" environment was affirming and nurturing for girls, but deprived boys of necessary challenge and competition.

The comment that the school's "soft" environment was more suited to girls' needs and thereby shortchanged boys disturbed me. Had we gone too far?

I had started the school in 1977 to create an ideal learning environment for all adolescents. The school's mission states: "To prepare students academically and personally for college and life in a rigorous educational environment that challenges them to think independently, respect individuality, and act with integrity." Did this mean different things for boys than for girls? Had I been blind to gender differences that necessitate different strategies? Yes, we were pretty sure that some strategies worked better with girls and others with boys. We saw that many girls responded better to a conversation, a dialogue. Many boys responded better to a direct, in-your-face, statement of insistence: "This is unacceptable," "Do this." But we also knew that there were exceptions to this rule. And we knew that all students, not just boys, needed clear, firm expectations, known consequences, and consistent accountability.

121

Reflecting on these issues led to the following entry in my personal journal:

> With gender, we used to view the differences among women and differences among men on separate scales. I believe that today we can put everyone on a common coed grid of traits—competitive, aggressive, physical strength, left brain preference and individualism, together with collaborative, relational, compliant, right brain and nurturing. The majority of women would be located in one region and the majority of men in another, but with lots of overlap. Such a grid would recognize traditional genetic "survival" characteristics and environmental, cultural influences and expectations. It would also recognize the uniqueness of each person, female and male.

Preparing young men and women for the gender complexity of the contemporary real world is a daunting task for schools and teachers. No two individual students, male, female, or nonbinary, will be at identical points on a grid of human personality and behavioral traits. The art of teaching resides to a great extent in intuitively knowing both when and what to do with each young person. Timing is critical—sensing when a student needs to be left alone, challenged, touched, encouraged, or told no. Good timing enables a teacher to be a catalyst in helping all students, regardless of gender, race, class or culture, to master a skill, understand an idea, or discover a new insight.

In February 2005, I received an email from Bruce, who had recently returned to Louisville. He was working a temporary job and having difficulty finding a desirable permanent job in the technology field, even with his strong credentials. When we met for lunch, I suggested a couple of possible leads, but the kind of position he was seeking has increasingly been outsourced to India. He was thinking of becoming an actuary. Bruce at twenty-six was more outgoing and comfortable with himself. I told him that I was writing about my experiences as an educator and planned to have a chapter inspired by gender issues. It would begin with his essay. How did he now feel about his "Chick Course" experience? "I never really liked the course," he said, "but I learned a lot from Ms. Bowman about reform movements." It would have been too much to expect for him to have added, "and about women," but I thought it for him.

# 15

## QUESTIONABLE ACCEPTANCE

The Admissions Committee was about to meet and I had just reviewed the folder of David Andrew, one of several applicants on today's agenda. We met in Abby's classroom down the hall from my office and Tim, Janey, and Bryan were already there when I arrived. They had each read David's folder. Janey rated him as "Clearly acceptable, aside from his behavior," Tim and Bryan as "Questionable," and Abby as "Not Acceptable."

Abby, a highly effective, super-organized French teacher, initiated the discussion.

"This kid will be a distraction to other students in most of his classes. We don't need him."

Tim, Dean of Students and history teacher, responded. "Actually Abby, we do need him. The incoming ninth grade so far is two-thirds girls. At this point we only have a couple of at-risk students in the class. Part of the problem besides immaturity is that David's bored. He has the potential and, in our small classes with more interesting teachers, it's likely he'll be more engaged."

I glanced at my notes from interviewing David: "Mechanically inclined, enjoys science and social studies, works for teachers he likes, a somewhat non-verbal, but not atypical eighth-grade boy.... Family data may explain the developmental issues David exhibits; he's the youngest of three children with two high achieving older sisters and both parents professionals with graduate degrees." David was clearly capable, but the decision was not straightforward.

We reached a consensus to accept David, but with the stipulation that he attend St. Francis' Preparation for Success course in August just prior to the start of the new school year. He completed the course, but his evaluation stated that, while David had the skills to be a successful high school student, he would need to apply himself more consistently. All new St. Francis students receive interim reports after four weeks of school. David's were predictable: "inconsistent homework," "lethargic in class," "occasionally not focused." I noted that he did better in courses where he had male teachers.

Two weeks later, counselor Janey came to see me about meeting with David's English teacher, Dan Beaufort. Ninth-grade English students kept journals in which they recorded personal responses to the literature they read. He was concerned about recent journal entries of Carol, who created graphic sexual fantasies, and David, who wrote about suicide. Janey gave Dan several suggestions and the two of them met with me the next day, a Friday. We decided that Janey would talk with Carol about her journal entries and confirm they were only fantasies. If not, she would determine if Carol was in an abusive or exploitative relationship.

Over half of adolescents have thoughts of suicide, but fewer than ten percent make an attempt, with three to four percent being successful. Suicidal thoughts are common, but attempts are serious calls for help. We concluded that David was not in a crisis, as we were unaware of any other risk factors being present. Dan would meet with him on Monday, discuss the journal entries, and report back to Janey and me. I asked him to add a note to his comments in David's journal saying he looked forward to seeing him Monday—a subtle message of a future and of his confidence in David. Dan returned the journal later that day and arranged the Monday meeting.

On a plane to a conference in Minneapolis the next day I thought about Dan's encouraging, affirming approach, which had motivated several disaffected students that other teachers had been unable to reach. But his tendency to get personally involved with students was also a potential problem. Dan met with David and satisfied Janey and me that the suicidal thoughts were not serious. From mid-October until late March, David stayed out of trouble and, except for failing history, managed his classes satisfactorily.

Parents often picked up students after school by pulling into the parking lot of the busy two-story McDonald's next door to the school. On March 22, Margaret Appleby was sitting in her car waiting for her son. She saw David, whom she recognized, take out of his wallet a tightly folded bill. Another boy, standing next to David, put down his backpack, took out a small plastic bag, and handed it to David. They quickly separated and went in opposite directions. When Mrs. Appleby got home, she called me about the exchange. I called David's mother, Janet, about the exchange and insisted that he be evaluated for drug use. She informed me David had recently admitted using marijuana and that she and her husband had made an appointment with Don Worth, a psychologist and drug counselor. David was suspended until Dr. Worth contacted the school with the results of his evaluation.

Janet called me two days later to report that David was depressed, was using marijuana to self-medicate, and had been hospitalized for treatment. He was prescribed an antidepressant, placed in individual and group therapy, and stayed for eleven days. After being discharged, he began weekly appointments with Dr. Worth. When

Don and I talked he told me that David was upbeat and had signed a contract that he would submit to random drug screens, was willing to remain drug free, and would attend daily Narcotics Anonymous meetings for ninety days.

Don confirmed that David was doing everything he was asked to do and recommended he return to school. A couple of days later David met with me. He clearly wanted to come back to school and I noticed that he had cut his shoulder-length hair. He described trying pot in seventh grade, not liking it, but in the eighth grade beginning to use with friends on weekends. Last summer he had smoked just a few times because he was working at a hospital. A couple of months after starting the ninth grade, he moved to daily use, mostly with his old friends from middle school. He didn't use during school; he had more sense than that. I thanked him for coming in and told him I would meet later that day with some of his teachers and then call his parents about readmittance.

Tim, Don, and I met during lunch. College counselor Fran Donnelly joined us. We decided that David be allowed to return and finish the year as long as he continued to comply with Dr. Worth's treatment plan. Tim would put together a set of expectations that David would have to meet to return for his sophomore year. I called David's father about our decision to let him finish the school year.

David returned and at first was uncharacteristically quiet. Then a week later, his P. E. teacher had to stop him from acting clownish during class. When I met with him, he explained he was on a new medication that made him feel dopey and sleepy. The next day his mother called me to say that his recent drug screen was negative, but that his medication was causing erratic behavior. During the remaining weeks of school. David was not disruptive, but was often sleepy, unfocused, and disinterested. He did manage to do sufficient work to pass all of his courses except history. He also complied with Dr. Worth's expectations for therapy, attending meetings, and passing periodic drug screens.

In June, one of my last appointments before I left for a six-month sabbatical leave was to discuss David's status with him and his parents. I told Mr. and Mrs. Andrew that based on his work and behavior since returning in April, we didn't see David being successful as a tenth grader at St. Francis. But since it was early in his recovery process, the school might reconsider later in the summer.

A month later in July, Tim met with David, who had recently completed working as an orderly at the University of Louisville Hospital. Tim had already received strongly positive recommendations from three hospital employees. David confirmed that he met with Dr. Worth weekly, went to group therapy every week, and attended regular NA meetings. He was excited about going to the National Guitar Summer Workshop in Connecticut for a week and talked about playing in a band with two friends. Tim noted that David seemed better, initiating conversation and making direct eye contact. He told David that once he received letters from teachers at the guitar camp, he would contact Dr. Worth, and convene the Admissions Committee, which would decide about readmission.

Tim received positive recommendations from the guitar workshop and, on August 6, had a lengthy phone conversation with Don Worth, who recommended that David be readmitted. He attested that David had improved with group interaction, was praised by group members, and had passed all urine tests. He believed that David deserved a second chance. With Dr. Worth's recommendation, Tim was ready to meet with the Admissions Committee. He expected them to approve David's readmittance, contingent on continued compliance with his contract with Dr. Worth.

That evening David and three friends made a decision that made the meeting irrelevant.

I was on an island in Penobscot Bay in Maine with two of my daughters and their families. The afternoon of August 7, a group of us were outside playing kickball. Someone called from the house that my wife Helen was on the phone. She told me that David, two other boys, and a girl, had been killed in a car wreck. It appeared that David had been driving. The accident happened on a foggy night around 3:00 am, when the car, going into a curve at excessive speed and for reasons that remain mysterious to this day, went out of control and flipped. The parents all thought their children were home asleep in bed. The four teenagers, none of them licensed drivers, had sneaked out for a joyride.

I hung up and stood by the phone. I thought about the four teenagers and about my grandchildren outside. I thought about Jim Hurst, my friend and colleague, Acting Head of School since I had left in June for my six-month sabbatical. Jim would be facing the families, newspaper reporters, and the school community—students, teachers, and parents. But I was not worried about his ability to handle such a difficult situation in my absence. Since starting the school together in 1977, we had weathered our fair share of tragedies and challenges.

I thought of David's parents, Janet and Scott, remembering the June meeting when I met with them about David's possible readmittance in September. They had worked hard to support David since his suspension from school and diagnosis as depressed and chemically dependent.

The day after the accident, Janet and Scott called to ask that the school posthumously readmit David based on his satisfactory compliance to date with the school's requirements. An unusual request, but why deny David's parents the solace and satisfaction of his summer accomplishments? Dan Beaufort wrote David a posthumous letter on behalf of the Admissions Committee and complimented him for the progress he had made and congratulated him on meeting the requirements for becoming a sophomore at St. Francis. The letter was sent to his parents and a copy placed in his school file.

I'll never know what prompted David to get behind the wheel of the automobile and take a midnight ride with his friends. I've learned a lot about adolescence in forty years of working with teenagers. When I began to write about David, I pulled out the yearbook from his freshman year to better remember him. He's in the front row of the group class photo, sweatshirt, jeans, fair complexion, unexceptional except for long blond hair flowing off his shoulders. But another photo from that October's Halloween party was unlike any other. His long hair is provocatively pulled over to one side, tattoo decals on forehead, and eyebrows and eyelashes heavily highlighted in black in homage to his idol, musician Kurt Cobain, who had recently killed himself..

Even at a school as small as St. Francis, I only ever see a small part of what makes each student a unique person. When I talked over the events of David's life with his parents many years later, I learned that we shared a love of old cars and that he preferred reading shop manuals to Shakespeare. His father told me David had singlehandedly rebuilt the single-barrel carburetor of a 1951 Chevrolet, a challenging task made all the more remarkable in that the car still runs today in that same repair. He had also repaired the scooter belonging to a young neighor. I learned that David used to share his lunch with a homeless man who spent every day on a nearby corner. I learned that after his death, several previously homeless persons had come up to David's father to let them know that David had helped them get jobs at the hospital.

And I learned that when David was looking at high schools with his parents, he had had a hard time. One school, he said, had too much fighting. At another, he would have to wear a tie, which felt constricting. When a family friend suggested they visit St. Francis, his parents told me, the moment he saw it, David told them, "No more schools. This is the place for me. They let you be a normal person."

Youth often explore who they are by differentiating themselves from parents and from their peers. Gaining maturity is a trial-and-error process and lapses of judgment are expected. We can only hope they don't have lasting or fatal consequences. Dan Beaufort's letter to David poignantly reminds those of us who work with teenagers that, no matter how much we reach out to them, their impulsiveness will often surprise us, disappoint us, and, sometimes, break our hearts:

My deepest regret is that I, and others who love you, will not have the chance to see the longer-term rewards of the strides you recently made. But that does not diminish in any way the fact that you made them. Because of that reality, my memory of you will be of the young man I saw pull his life together in a successful and rewarding way. I thank you for showing us that our faith in you was not mistaken, that you were a strong, talented, intelligent, and kind human being.

# 16

---

## LEO

In a progressive school with a hundred and forty adolescents and several dozen staff members, I could expect each day to bring something surprising, exciting, and often troublesome.

One morning in October, 1995, surprise and challenge for me were triggered by Steve, a French teacher. A majority of his student evaluations expressed concern about his being poorly prepared for class; unless he showed significant improvement, he was unlikely to continue teaching at St. Francis.

I was walking down the first floor hallway when Steve stepped out of the French classroom and asked if we could talk for a minute.

"Tom, when I came in the front door there was the usual stack of *LEO*s. I decided that I finally had to tell you how I feel about *LEO*. Has it ever occurred to you that *LEO* may give visitors the wrong impression of St. Francis?"

I was about to respond, "And what impression would that be, Steve?" but caught myself. The tone of his voice was serious, and knowing my liberal proclivities, his raising the issue took some courage.

"What about *LEO*'s content seems inappropriate to you? Sure, its editorial stance is even left of the *Courier-Journal*'s, but St. Francis students understand editorial bias."

"It's not politics or the irreverent tone that bothers me, Tom. It's the ads inside the back cover. They're offensive to me personally, but, more important, I don't think they're suitable for teenagers."

Steve was referring to the last page of the classified ads, which used innovative fonts to promote massage therapists (*MAGIC HANDS* by Laura at Spa Fantasia), relaxation sessions (Come Relax With Tiffany), and clubs (PT's SHOWCLUB, COME SEE WHAT YOU'VE BEEN MISSING! and *RUSTIC FROG*: THE MOST BEAUTIFUL GIRLS, 2 for 1 Couch Dance Specials). I was certain every student knew they were there—teenagers are relentlessly fascinated by adult sexuality. But I trusted them to decide for themselves what they wanted to know and to learn to evaluate what they read and saw in the adult world.

The *Louisville Eccentric Observer*, known as *LEO*, is a free, weekly, alternative newspaper, distributed every Wednesday to over eight hundred locations in the Louisville area. Back when Steve questioned its suitability, a bundle of *LEO*s was left once a week just inside the school's front door.

*LEO* is devoted to opinion, commentary, and reviews, mostly written by local writers. It also carries nationally syndicated features like the *New York Times* crossword puzzle and "News of the Weird." As a free paper, *LEO* is wholly supported by advertising, with only one or two of fifty pages containing the ads which upset Steve. *LEO*'s lively, offbeat, iconoclastic style made it regular reading by many teachers and students. St. Francis had become a distribution point three years earlier when I okayed a teacher's request as a convenience for those who enjoyed reading it.

I told Steve that this was the first time that anyone had complained about *LEO*, but he had raised an important issue. Still, being available in the school's lobby didn't mean that anyone was required to read it.

"Picking up a copy is an individual decision. I would give permission for a free conservative weekly if a request were made. But you're right that having *LEO* in the lobby could give the impression to both students and visitors that the school approves of its contents."

"That's what I'm worried about, Tom. Its being in the school's lobby is likely to offend others as well as me."

"All right, Steve, I'll bring up the issue at the upcoming staff meeting and then take it to the School Committee. Don't worry, I won't say who brought it to my attention."

In letting the School Committee decide the issue, I would again test my confidence and trust in the emerging adult always present in teenagers. Expecting and affirming adult behavior from adolescents while having clear expectations and consequences in response to immature actions is central to St. Francis High School's developmental philosophy.

At the staff meeting I reported that someone had questioned St. Francis being a distribution point for *LEO*, referring to the "adult only" ads inside the back cover. I started a discussion by asking several questions. "In making *LEO* available, are we condoning the ads? Does providing *LEO* send an unintended and undesired message about the school's values? Should St. Francis continue to be a distribution site?"

There were around twenty-five of us, mostly teachers, plus the small administrative staff. We were sitting around pulled-together tables in the Commons Room on the third floor. At the end of a school day spent with energetic teenagers, we were tired and the room was hot. But I could see and sense interest in their faces and the meeting minutes reflect the lively discussion that followed.

"*LEO* is available, but we aren't really distributing it—some people choose to take a copy; others ignore the paper."

"We help students develop values and then trust them to act in a responsible manner."

"Having *LEO* available shows we are tolerant and non-reactionary."

"Should we consider having a media literacy course as part of the curriculum?"

"How does the school approach sexuality? Does providing *LEO* in the school convey a message that we approve of aspects of sexuality expressed by some of the ads, especially submission, domination, and exploitation of women?"

"Are we doing all we can to help students develop healthy sexuality? Is it our role to do this? If yes, what can we do that is effective?"

"There was a recent *LEO* editorial about why these ads were accepted."

"Let's invite the publisher to come and meet with us."

The next day I called John Yarmuth at *LEO* and told him about the staff's discussion. He graciously agreed to meet with the School Committee and interested teachers. John, a Louisville native and graduate of Yale University, had worked in Washington for a Kentucky senator for several years before returning to Louisville to begin a career in publishing. He founded *LEO* in 1990 and continued to write a regular column until he entered politics and won a seat in the U.S. House of Representatives in 2006.

A week later John met with the School Committee and its advisor Tim Marshall, who moderated the discussion. To alert the School Committee to the special agenda and guest, I sent a memo to each of the thirteen members—four seniors and three students from each of the lower grades, elected by their classmates.

That school year, 1995-1996, only two of the thirteen members of the School Committee were boys. Confident that the empowered young women in the group would be a good match for *LEO*'s publisher, I looked forward to the exchange. An important part of the school's approach to college preparation is to provide opportunities for students to engage adult issues, in this case freedom of choice and speech.

The meeting took place in a classroom on the third floor, with everyone sitting around a cluster of tables. A visitor unfamiliar with the school would have been struck by the contrast between the casual appearance of students, dressed in jeans, t-shirts, and sweaters, and the interest and alertness in their faces and posture.

John began by saying that he was pleased to have been invited and that he was familiar with St. Francis High School and impressed with its commitment to being downtown. He understood that there were concerns about *LEO* being distributed at St. Francis and asked for questions. I was not surprised that the first question came from Liz, an assertive, bright, and confident senior, encouraged by her lawyer parents.

The dialogue was contentious from the beginning, but respectful. What follows is a re-creation from my notes.

"Mr. Yarmuth, I'm Liz Goldstein and I enjoy reading *LEO* until I get to the last couple of pages. Please tell me why you accept ads which blatantly support the exploitation of women?"

"Liz, as a regular reader, you probably saw my editorial last month addressing these ads, which are just part of the classified ad section at the back of every issue. Obviously my response did not satisfy you. I gave two reasons, one based on my long-standing belief in freedom of expression. These businesses are engaged in legal activities. Their employees have freely chosen to work in them. Why should the businesses not be allowed to advertise? You may see exploitation, but others see opportunity. Readers who object to the ads are free not to read them, just as readers who disagree with my editorials can skip them and go to the crossword puzzle. It's advertising, including the ads in question, that makes *LEO* free, an important reason for its circulation of 150,000 and probably why you and many students read it."

"I understand your reasons, Mr. Yarmuth, but if the publisher, editor, and majority of readers were women, not men, would these ads be in *LEO*?"

"That's tough, Liz, but I would have to say no, if the women were as informed and passionate as you are."

Mina, gentle, compassionate, and equally informed as Liz, spoke next. "I'm Mina Gupta, a junior member of the School Committee. Mr. Pike wants us to make a recommendation about the school continuing to be a *LEO* distribution site. My parents send me to St. Francis because of its excellent academic program. But they are conservative and would be upset if they knew I read your paper. I'm not sure they would have let me enroll here if they had seen a stack of *LEO*s in the office when we visited the school. Teachers have expressed concern that providing *LEO* conveys the message that the school endorses your liberal editorial stance and is okay with the activities advertised. What do you think?"

"I suspect that most parents who are considering St. Francis for their kids already know that it is a progressive school that attracts bright, independent thinking students. Seeing a pile of *LEO*s would not bother them. These parents would know enough about St. Francis not to assume the school endorsed the ads. Most conservative parents would probably never have read a *LEO* and seen the ads. Besides, freedom of expression includes the freedom of choosing not to read or listen to things that offend you."

Joe, one of the two boys on the School Committee, a classic high-achiever with the drive and intelligence to accomplish anything he wanted to do, jumped in. "Mr. Yarmuth, responsible newspaper publishers have guidelines for both news stories and advertisements. Why doesn't the *Courier-Journal* accept ads like the ones we're talking about?"

"Good question, Joe. The *Courier-Journal*, while its editorial stance is liberal, is a mainstream daily newspaper seeking a broad readership. Unlike *LEO*, they don't publish columnists like Molly Ivins or features like "News of the Weird." Their paid circulation is state-wide and ten times larger than *LEO*'s. We are a local, free, urban weekly with an openly eccentric approach seeking compatible readers, whether libertarian, centrist, or liberal, and our policies reflect that readership."

The rest of the meeting continued in a similar vein. The students clearly understood John's explanations, but as I watched and listened I sensed that the majority, especially the girls, were not satisfied. When the forty-minute session was over, John complimented the students for the quality of their questions. He told them that they were better informed than most of the adult audiences he addressed and that coming to St. Francis was much more fun than speaking at the Rotary Club.

John obviously enjoyed the exchange and kids like Liz, Mina, and Joe were allowed, encouraged to do exactly what students should be doing in schools: using their heads and hearts to foster challenge and growth. I recently asked John, who at time of writing had represented Kentucky's 3rd district in Congress since 2006, about the episode. He told me that he remembered the day fondly, and that his respect for the students of St. Francis had grown exponentially from the experience.

I was delighted that the three most outspoken students were Catholic, Hindu, and Jewish, enrolled at a progressive independent school named for a rebellious thirteenth century Italian teenager, who questioned the cultural norms of his time.

The next day at Morning Meeting, I described the meeting with

John and asked all students to tell their representatives on the School Committee how they felt regarding the distribution of *LEO* at St. Francis.

The School Committee met the following week to decide on their recommendation. After the meeting, advisor Tim Marshall and I talked for a while about the Committee's decision that the school continue to be a *LEO* distribution point. He was proud of the students, both for their impressive questioning of John Yarmuth and their conclusion that freedom of expression was more important than individual reservations about the ads.

It seemed natural at the time to leave this decision to the students, regardless of the consequences. Looking back, I'm amazed at the many risks I took in trusting my own instincts as an educator. In encouraging kids to be creative, to naturally seek growth as unique, emerging adults, I learned over and over again that clear expectations, trust, and love for these kids are essential. They create an environment that nourishes the kind of learning, both personal and intellectual, that I wished I had experienced in high school. And, nearly always, the risks were worth it.

In 2003 *LEO* was sold to a national publishing company, and in 2008 was upgraded with a new logo and slick magazine paper instead of newsprint. *LEO* is still a free weekly alternative magazine, with the usual features and a page or two of "adult only" ads inside the back cover. But *LEO*s now have their own distribution kiosk on the corner of Third and Broadway, about thirty feet from St. Francis High School's main entrance. The decision was made by the current publisher, not the school or the students.

# 17

## THE "N" WORD

Mattie Jones' phone call caught me by surprise.

"Tom, I don't like some of the short stories that Alyssa's English teacher has assigned. They disturb and confuse her. Having read one called 'Powerhouse,' I don't blame her. Alyssa also told me that several other stories used the word [here Mattie quoted the "N-word"] which bothered her. These stories are not appropriate for teenagers and I'm appalled by your insensitivity to the school's few African-American students. You and St. Francis need to make some changes. I've talked to Louis Coleman and we want to meet with you, Mr. Beaufort, and Alyssa. Joe McMillan from U of L is coming with us. When can we get together?"

I caught my breath and glanced at my calendar.

We settled on Wednesday and, as I hung up the phone, I was as disturbed as Alyssa's grandmother. St. Francis had struggled for years to attract and retain African-American students. Our efforts would be severely sabotaged if I were unable to satisfy Mattie Jones and her activist colleagues. But I was equally determined not to undermine St. Francis' traditions of academic freedom and challenging its college-bound students with provocative, sophisticated material.

I had two days to prepare for the meeting, including talks with Dan Beaufort and Alyssa. I met first with Dan, who had been at St. Francis since its founding in 1977. Casual in appearance, Dan's once long, thick hair was now thin and clipped and his shaggy, full beard trimmed. While obviously irritated by what he felt was an unnecessary meeting, he was ready to justify his choice of Eudora Welty's story and describe how he prepared the class to read "Powerhouse."

Dan explained that he assigned the class to write at least two pages in their English sketchbook in response to each of the nine stories in the short story unit. Then during class he randomly chose students to read their comments aloud. Among the stories were three by African-American writers—Langston Hughes, Ann Petry and Alice Walker—and one by West Indian writer Merle Hodge. He knew that Alyssa did not like to read in front of her classmates and told me that he had begun to alert her ahead of time that he would be calling on her. As she did not always do her homework, he hoped this would motivate her to be better prepared. I asked Dan to tell Alyssa about Wednesday's meeting and that she needed to meet with me.

"You wanted to see me, Mr. Pike?" A subdued Alyssa stood in the doorway. She wasn't the sort of student to cause problems, and I felt sure that this was the first time she had been summoned to a principal's office. She had enrolled in St. Francis' tenth grade after completing the ninth grade at Scribner Junior High School, a large public school in Southern Indiana, across the river from Louisville. A tall, fit, three-season athlete and popular teenager but an average student, Alyssa struggled to keep up with her schoolwork. Like many transfers, she was not accustomed to the higher expectations of teachers and the closer, more personalized attention at St. Francis. These, of course, were the main reasons her mother and grandmother had enrolled her. Alyssa had been content at her previous school where she didn't have to work hard and where there were many African-American students. I suspected that part of her complaint to her mother and grandmother was an attempt to have them reconsider their decision to send her to St. Francis.

Alyssa told me that she wasn't a good reader and didn't like to read out loud. She complained that Mr. Beaufort kept calling on her. As the only Black student in the class, it seemed that he would always choose her whenever a story dealt with African Americans. She also said that many of the stories, like "Powerhouse," were hard for her to write about in her sketchbook.

"Tell me about your difficulties with Eudora Welty's complex story 'Powerhouse.'" Alyssa said she was upset by the crude portrayal of the Black piano player in the words of a naive narrator, a young woman in the all-white audience at the club where Powerhouse and his band were playing. Alyssa had told her mother and grandmother that she didn't like "Powerhouse." She had read some of it to them.

I picked up a copy of her anthology, *Points of View*, and asked her to show me what she had read.

Powerhouse is playing! ... There's no one in the world like him. You can't tell what he is. "Negro man?" —he looks more Asiatic monkey, Jewish, Babylonian, Peruvian, fanatic, devil. He has pale gray eyes, heavy lids. Maybe horny like a lizard's, but big glowing eyes when they're open. ... He's not coal black—beverage color—looks like a preacher when his mouth is shut, but then it opens—vast and obscene. And his mouth is going every minute: like a monkey's when it looks for something.

It might make sense in the context of Welty's story, but this was definitely not a paragraph a Black student should have been asked to read out loud in class.

One reason I had founded an independent, non-public school was to have the freedom to hire any teachers I believed could engage and inspire teenagers, regardless of certification or experience. Although the ninth grade short story unit was new to Dan, he was used to teaching interesting and challenging material. The short stories assigned were from *Points of View*, by James Moffett. Originally published in 1966, it was an anthology typically used in colleges and universities, with selections reflecting a variety of ethnicities and social classes.

When we met that Wednesday, Alyssa sat nervously on my right; on my left was Dan Beaufort, grim but determined. Across from us were three of Louisville's most prominent Black activists: Mattie Jones of the Kentucky Alliance Against Racist and Political Repression, the Reverend Louis Coleman, founder and director of the Justice Resource Center, and Joe McMillan, Chair of the University of Louisville's Department of Pan-African Studies. I had not previously met Joe, but over the years I had participated in some of the many public rallies Mattie and Louis had organized to protest unjust treatment of members of Louisville's African American community.

Mattie Jones had been a civil rights activist since the 1960s, when she had marched with Martin Luther King Jr. in Louisville against segregation in public schools and for open housing. She and I had met over these issues at St. Francis High School before, as well. In 1988, St. Francis had been the site of a debate between an anti-apartheid activist from the University of Louisville and a visiting white diplomat from South Africa. A similar debate had been held a few days earlier at a public high school but was disrupted by Mattie and other protestors. They had burst onto the stage, seized the microphone, sung anti-apartheid songs, and yelled slogans. Their disruption caused another school to cancel its debate altogether. I decided to invite the protestors to join the debate at St. Francis and express their views, provided they allowed the two lead speakers the same courtesy. Mattie had agreed, and she and her group stood at the back of the room holding signs against apartheid. When the two main speakers finished, she and another protestor spoke briefly.

Ironically, the diplomat turned out to be a moderate. He surprised the audience by freely admitting that institutionalized discrimination such as apartheid was wrong. "Apartheid is dead. It's just a question of what to do with the rotting corpse." He went on to describe the government's plans for desegregation and the difficulties involved because of the number of tribes with conflicting views and agendas. Students peppered him with questions about the slow pace of the government's actions. The lively and informative program had been a victory for free speech, encouraged and valued at St. Francis. Mattie also had seemed satisfied with the result, and I was very pleased when her granddaughter enrolled at St. Francis a few years later.

I introduced Dan to Mattie and Joe and thanked them for coming. Mattie said that Louis was on his way but would be late as usual. Louis' mission helping his people was a twenty-four-hour job, whether on the street picketing, in corporate offices requesting jobs and grants, or at the police station seeking justice. Most of the folks he irritated begrudgingly admired his courage and perseverance. I suggested we start by having Dan explain his choice of Welty's story. He first apologized to Alyssa for whatever discomfort he had caused her. He told her that it was not his intent to upset her, but for his students to learn to understand and respond to different kinds of literature. Alyssa was subdued, and perhaps a bit embarrassed. She had not anticipated her complaints causing such a meeting. At this point Louis arrived, apologetic, disheveled, and looking as if he had been up all night, which it turned out he had. Alyssa was excused to go to her next class and Dan began to explain why and how he taught these stories.

He described introducing "Powerhouse" to his students by setting it in its time and place—the late 1930s, in the South, an all-white audience listening to a charismatic Black piano player. He pointed out Eudora Welty's unusual use of two narrative voices, an unnamed young white woman revealing her conflicted racial attitudes and a second omniscient observer taking the reader into the defiant, triumphant mind of Powerhouse. In subsequent discussions of the story, he led students to see that Welty was deliberately challenging readers to examine their own prejudices. He noted how she depicted the white narrator as ignorant and unconsciously racist and the piano player as noble and talented. Louis and Joe listened with interest; Mattie was agitated and impatient.

Dan further explained that his white students needed to learn to recognize racism if it was ever to cease. Louis and Joe both seemed to understand how Dan had prepared his students for reading the story and to accept his reasons for assigning it. When Louis left for another meeting, he said to Joe and Mattie, "We don't have to worry about this boy, he's all right."

But Mattie was adamant that stories like "Powerhouse," even Mark Twain's *The Adventures of Huckleberry Finn*, should not be assigned to high school students. Both Mattie and Joe lamented the lack of efforts at St. Francis to explore African-American culture and the poor job the school did recruiting and retaining African-American students and teachers.

"Tom, you've got to make some changes. Your teachers and students must be more sensitive to racial issues. You need to have diversity training for the whole school as well as workshops for the staff. You need help; Louis and I will be glad to work with you."

I responded. "We're open to having workshops on diversity,

Mattie, and welcome your help and participation. But an essential, unique part of St. Francis' educational philosophy is using materials that are provocative and instructive regarding gender, racial, and political issues. For me to prohibit teachers from assigning specific literary works would contradict the school's mission. I trust our teachers to appropriately introduce such materials as Dan clearly did with Welty's story."

Mattie and Joe accepted my stance and the tone of the meeting shifted from confrontation to cooperation. We explored various possibilities for workshops and discussed strategies for recruiting minority students and faculty. I agreed to have an all-day, all-school prejudice reduction workshop before the end of school and a faculty-staff workshop in August before the start of the next school year. Both Mattie and Joe agreed to help St. Francis attract African-American staff and students and Mattie offered to lead the staff workshop. She promised to arrange for Louis Coleman and Anne Braden, a Louisville-based, nationally known white civil rights activist, to be co-leaders.

Two weeks later, I recounted the meeting with Mattie, Louis, and Joe with St. Francis' English and history teachers. One reason they teach in a progressive independent school is to be able to design their own courses and choose the texts they want to teach, subject only to my oversight as Head of School. Having this freedom benefited their students, as classes tended to be livelier and more engaging. As I expected, the teachers became angry. "Jesus Christ, Tom. You mean they wouldn't even let us teach Huck Finn." Everyone settled down when I made clear that I wasn't about to change St. Francis' twenty-five-year tradition of trusting teachers to select appropriate texts. I did remind them of their responsibility to provide students whatever background was necessary to understand what they were being required to read.

The discussion shifted to the difficulty of teaching materials dealing with racism with only one or two Black students in the room. Sensitivity to minority students was essential. Most important was not putting a minority student on the spot by treating them as an expert witness and interpreter, as Alyssa felt had happened in Dan's class. Equally problematic was addressing homosexuality with just one or two gay or lesbian students in a class. Teachers should consider meeting individually with reticent or potentially exposed students like Alyssa to explain why they were teaching controversial material and reach an understanding about when and how to call on that student.

Later in May, I brought in a team of facilitators from the National Coalition Building Institute to lead the all-day prejudice reduction workshop for the school. Students were divided into small groups, diverse in age, gender, size, shape, race, ethnicity, religion, neighborhood, and socio-economic level. Stereotypes and prejudices were examined, confronted, and diffused through a number of different activities. A non-threatening atmosphere was created for students to become aware of the prejudices, which unconsciously shaped their responses to other students. Unfortunately, Alyssa chose not to continue at St. Francis; nevertheless, I hoped we could learn and improve based on what had happened as a consequence of her complaint.

Mattie and Louis came back at the end of August with Anne Braden and led two sessions of diversity training for the staff. Their words heightened our sensitivity to how it felt for a solitary Black student to be in a class of white kids taught by white teachers. In the years since the "N" word incident, the number of African-American students at St. Francis has more than doubled. Twenty-five percent of the student body are now students of color, most of them African American, ensuring that none of them will be alone in a class of white kids. In January, 2020, at the age of 87, Mattie Jones was honored with the Mayor's 2020 Dr. Martin

Luther King Jr. Freedom Award winner. She was profiled in the *Courier-Journal* for her "more than six decades of activism ... countless demonstrations, public conversations and boycotts focused on women's and workers' rights, environmental justice and police brutality." The headline of the article reads, "How a Louisville woman helped shape the city's civil rights movement. She's not done yet." Nor are we.

# 18

## ESTHER

She stood among the other ninth graders at St. Francis High School's freshman orientation, listening to an explanation of the first activity. When Dean of Students Tim Marshall finished, Esther raised her hand and asked a question that he had already answered. Throughout the many orientation activities, she continued to ask unnecessary questions. Esther was skinny, with straggly, blond hair and a prominent nose, her voice loud and demanding, magnifying a slight speech impediment. Inept socially and physically clumsy, by the end of the day she had established herself as a nuisance to both classmates and teachers—a bound-to-be rejected fifteen-year-old. I knew her time at St. Francis wouldn't be easy for any of us. I felt sorry for her then, but I would grow to like and respect her.

Once back at school, I pulled Esther's file, curious to learn about her history. It had been a year since the admissions interview, but I immediately remembered her background. She had been an atypical admissions applicant, with widely scattered test scores, average grades, and learning difficulties due to attention deficit disorder (non-hyperactive) and neurologic apraxia, which affects speech, motor skills, information processing, and organizational ability. Diagnosed as a young child, Esther had received extensive, ongoing therapy and counseling, and, like a good number of students over the years, her behavior would also have been affected by medication. She was one of five daughters of professional parents, who had obviously worked hard to support their middle child in acquiring the skills and fortitude to function in the mainstream. When I had interviewed her, Esther surprised and impressed me with her confidence, ambition, and independent spirit. She described herself as sensitive, outgoing and artistic. When asked about outgoing, she told me about not being afraid to raise her hand in class, to talk to someone whom she didn't know, or to make friends with many different types of people. "Mr. Pike," she said to me, "I have never perceived myself as handicapped."

The Admissions Committee voted unanimously to accept Esther, based on her spirit, willingness to persevere, and ninetieth percentile scores on a recent battery of achievement tests, which she had been allowed to take untimed. Her older sister, Henrietta, a current St. Francis senior, had been academically and socially successful, and her parents made clear that they would provide any extra support Esther needed.

During her four years at St. Francis, Esther learned to soften her aggressive attitude. While never becoming part of a clique, she had several friends and gained the respect of classmates by volunteering for jobs they didn't want to do and then doing them well. Teachers admired her tenacity and hard work, but found teaching her frustrating. Esther drove them crazy with endless questions, but managed to meet course expectations, often earning a 'B' rather than the expected 'C'.

I taught Esther in Finite Mathematics, an applied math course, which included probability and statistics. I had realized twenty-five years earlier that being involved in the design, implementation, and oversight of learning was a better fit for my talents than full-time teaching. But I missed the challenge and satisfaction of teaching math to teenagers and usually taught one course per semester. There were thirteen students in Esther's class, all seniors, with a wide range of abilities and learning styles. Each day was an absorbing test of my ability to keep them productively engaged. Some had little or no interest in math. Many took the class just to have four years of mathematics courses on their transcripts. Two students, Bobby and Mark, understood the material more quickly than most of the other students and were easily bored. They should have been in AP Calculus, but had not earned a place in the advanced class.

The risk and the drama of teaching is the unpredictability of each day's class, no matter how well prepared the teacher. I never knew when Mark and Bobby would act out, show off, or make subtle, disparaging comments about the obtuseness of some of their less able classmates, often behind my back. They knew I was frustrated, which only raised the stakes of the game we played. My success with teenagers was based on an underlying affection and respect for them, which provided a healthy, constructive framework for discipline. But in Mark's and Bobby's arrogance and sense of entitlement, I found little to like or respect. Throughout the first semester I struggled to prevent the two boys from disrupting other students' learning and my teaching.

The first class after the Martin Luther King Jr. holiday weekend went from bad to worse as the period progressed. I was at the blackboard introducing a new, complicated topic—one Bobby and Mark had previously covered. Had I remembered that my presentation would be review for them, I could have excused them to work on the next day's homework assignment. Instead, I plowed ahead with a series of examples the rest of the class needed. I heard

Bobby groan and looked right at him.

"That's enough, Bobby, be quiet."

"I didn't say a word, Mr. Pike," he retorted with a grin on his face.

"You know exactly what I mean. Just keep quiet."

A couple of minutes later, I responded to a question from Esther. I had grown to like this idiosyncratic learner who often needed a different kind of explanation. Teaching Esther was a challenge, because she kept questioning me until I came up with an example that worked. But this was okay because I had learned that the quieter, more reticent students benefited from the additional examples prompted by Esther's assertiveness.

"Look at it this way. The probability of an event happening depends on the conditions. Take a card example. If you drew a card from a normal deck of fifty-two cards, what would be the probability of drawing a heart?"

"That's easy, thirteen over fifty-two." Esther picked up her calculator and carefully, slowly punched in the numbers. "That's twenty-five percent."

"Okay, but suppose the conditions change and you know that the deck is missing two cards, one of them a heart. The probability of drawing a heart in this case is what we call a conditional probability because you have additional information about the deck which changes the calculation."

Let me see, there are now twelve hearts and fifty cards. So the ratio is twelve over fifty."

As she reached again for her calculator, I saw Mark and Bobby roll their eyes at each other, sigh loudly, and, under their breath, say, "Come on, Esther," attracting the attention of the other students.

At this point, after months of frustration in dealing with their disruptive behavior, I overreacted, yelled at both boys, and threatened to send them to the Discipline Review Board, the school's student jury. I gained control over the class, but lost any chance of creating a positive learning climate. We struggled through the balance of the class period.

The next day, I came straight to class from a meeting of the Board of Directors. My morning had been so crammed that I had no time to review what I was going to teach. I took several minutes to express disappointment in myself and Bobby and Mark for the previous day's poor class. I reminded the students that everyone was responsible for an atmosphere of productive and respectful learning.

Esther's hand went up.

"Yes, Esther?"

She explained with her typical directness where I had gone wrong in my responses to the boy's disrespectful behavior.

"Mr. Pike, we all know that Bobby and Mark can be pains in the butt, but you let them egg you on until you lost it. They've been bugging you all year. Don't mess around with them. Give them one warning, and if they don't quit, send them to the DRB. And you guys, so you're bored some of the time. It's your own fault you're in this class. Stop being spoiled brats and grow up if you ever expect to survive college."

We moved through the balance of the period in a buoyant flow of give and take. Esther was so breathtakingly on target it took all of us by surprise, including Mark and Bobby. The class mood was magically transformed. Sometimes it's the students, and not the teachers, who make everything work out.

# 19

## THE COUNTERFEIT CAPER

The Louisville spring was lush with white and pink blossomed dogwoods and newly green leafed maples and oaks. We had recovered from hectic Kentucky Derby Week with its Mardi Gras atmosphere. Final exams were in two weeks, followed by graduation and the end of another school year. I was in my office, feeling relaxed, when a call came from Special Agent Kent Burnell of the United States Department of Treasury.

"Mr. Pike," his voice authoritative yet pleasant, "Since early March, I have been investigating the spending of counterfeit twenty-dollar bills at a number of Louisville area businesses, several near the school. I have evidence of the involvement of six St. Francis students in making and passing the bills." He told me that he would be at the school in an hour to interview each of them, probably taking about forty-five minutes per student. At my request, he agreed to let Tim Marshall also be present. I learned early in my career as an educator to have a trusted colleague sit in on potentially problematic meetings, a help in reconstructing accurately what took place.

I listened intently as Mr. Burnell told me the names of the six boys involved—three ninth graders, one tenth grader, one junior, and one senior. None of them were close friends. A diverse group—some academically strong, some average students; some were athletes, others not. Several were affluent and two received significant financial aid grants. Four had never been in trouble before; one had a record of minor infractions. The sixth boy had a previous major offense and had already been denied re-enrollment for the coming school year.

Kent (we quickly got on a first name basis) disclosed some of the details as to how he had identified the boys. Security cameras had captured images of them as they spent the bills. Several of the twenties had been spent at the McDonald's next door to the school and the manager and workers identified the boys involved as St. Francis students. Concluding that the perpetrators were probably all St. Francis students, Kent easily identified the six boys, as St. Francis only had a hundred and thirty students, boys and girls. He had already met with one of the boys and his father and knew who made the bills.

"Making and passing counterfeit bills is a federal offense, a felony," he informed me. "Guilty individuals eighteen years or older are typically sentenced from six months to five years in a federal prison with no parole. Minors can also be prosecuted." Fortunately, Kent's first priority was to locate the bills and remove them from circulation. If the students cooperated and reimbursed the businesses for their losses, the government would not prosecute.

I hung up the phone and sat quietly at my desk, letting my mind sort through what Kent had told me. While this incident was unique, thirty-six years of working in schools had given me lots of practice with difficult, complicated situations. Although this was the only visit I would receive from a Secret Service agent, every few years, we would be visited by an officer of the law. I loved the challenges these incidents provided, especially the personal, human dimension to school problems that increased the complexity and appeal of my work. In this case, I would need to craft a solution that met the developmental needs of six different adolescents and ensured the survival of a school community placed at risk by their actions. It was unlikely that the incident could be kept a secret. A progressive high school in an educationally conservative community, St. Francis already had the reputation of being unconventional. A story on the TV evening news or in the local newspaper could seriously jeopardize the school's future. Fortunately, the government shared the school's desire to keep the incident from becoming public. They did not want it known how easy it was to make passable counterfeit twenties. With care and some luck, St. Francis might avoid making the front page of the Louisville *Courier-Journal*.

I knew all of the students fairly well. Neither dumb nor devious, they were just teenagers whose non-thinking actions had put our school in jeopardy and were going to cost me a couple of days' work.

I buzzed Lucy, my assistant and the school's receptionist. "Please cancel my appointments for the rest of the day. I'm expecting a Mr. Burnell in about thirty minutes. He, Tim, and I will be meeting with some students. Do your best to keep things quiet as I know you can. I'll explain later."

With his well-tailored suit, professional demeanor, and precise speech, Special Agent Kent Burnell could easily have been a corporate lawyer. With the help of Lucy and Tim, Kent interviewed the six boys without creating turmoil in the school. But I knew it was only a matter of time before the news would be out. My brain continued to focus on how to minimize the potential damage to the school and deal effectively not only with the boys but with their parents, who could be counted upon to react in diverse ways, some supportive, some not.

We met in my office, sitting in a cluster of four chairs, as I preferred to talk to people without the barrier of a desk between us. Sounds of car exhausts, loud boom boxes, and pedestrian voices from Third Street filtered through the row of clerestory windows along the top of the office's exterior wall. When one of the boys came in with Tim, he saw first me and then Kent on my right.

Dave was a doctor's son, a good soccer player, and a 'B' student. He was under a lot of pressure from his parents to earn good grades and gain admission to a prestigious college. Kent wanted to interview him first to confirm Jack's role as maker of the bills. According to Kent, Dave had helped Jack sell the bills to the other students and Jack had shared the proceeds with him. Dave's involvement was a surprise, as I had never considered him a risk-taker.

"Dave, this is Mr. Burnell, who is investigating a case for the Department of Treasury and needs to ask you some questions. Sit down and we'll get started."

"I'm a Secret Service Special Agent and the case I am investigating involves a group of students making and spending counterfeit twenty-dollar bills. This is a federal felony and minors can be prosecuted. I have evidence that you are one of the students involved."

Dave was his usual clean-cut self, short hair, casually but neatly dressed. He was calm and ready to respond to being questioned. Predictably, he had decided his best chance to avoid serious consequences was to cooperate and try to minimize his participation.

"What do you want to know?"

"Who made the bills and what was your role in distributing them?"

"Jack Stewart made them on his computer. When the word got out that he was selling them for five dollars, George McClellan asked me to get him some and gave me money to buy them." Dave added that he gave the money to Jack, who gave him five dollars and a roll of bills for George.

"Who else bought bills from Jack?"

"Ted Wortham and Mike Larson. Jack kept them in a little black bag—rolls of one-hundred-dollars-worth with rubber bands around them. They seemed to be everywhere. Yesterday, I found a roll of ten bills and flushed it down the toilet. This morning I found another roll of five twenties under an algebra book and threw it out a window,"

"You mean that you never kept or used any of the bills," asked Kent, his skepticism obvious.

"No, Mr. Burnell, I never spent any of them. I've got more sense than that. My parents would have a fit and a felony on my record would totally screw up my chances to attend a good college."

Standing up, Kent thanked Dave for his cooperation. "Mr. Pike and I will be contacting your parents. Do not talk to anyone about this. The success of my investigation depends on keeping things quiet."

As Dave left, I told him that he was suspended for today, tomorrow, and Monday. Also, that Tim Marshall and I would meet with him and his parents on Monday to inform them of additional consequences. He left, subdued and worried.

Tim went to get Jack, whose leading role in the incident puzzled me. He was one of the hardest-working, highest-achieving students in the school and a dedicated runner, number one on the cross-country team. I knew Jack better than most students, as he was a member of the School Committee, St. Francis' student council, and we were often in meetings together. Raised by a single mother whose life revolved around him, he had received a full scholarship since he arrived as a ninth grader. His involvement was the biggest surprise of all.

Tim came back in with Jack, who appeared his typically serious, contained self. I introduced Jack to Kent and we all sat down.

"Jack, I'm investigating a case for the Department of Treasury.

It involves a group of six St. Francis students making, selling, and spending counterfeit twenty-dollar bills. This is a felony and minors can be prosecuted. I have learned that you are one of the students involved."

Jack looked right at me, composed and steady, sitting ramrod straight, "Mr. Pike, you know me. You know I wouldn't be involved in something like counterfeiting."

"Listen to Mr. Burnell, Jack. You wouldn't be here if he did not have compelling evidence. Your cooperation could keep you from being prosecuted."

Kent continued, "I know from several sources that you made the bills. The government's main goal is to locate all the bills and you have information that will help me. It's not too late to cooperate. I need to know how many you made, to whom you sold or gave them, and how many you still have."

"You must be mistaken," Jack answered coolly, "You have the wrong person. I don't know what other students have told you, but I am not involved in counterfeiting."

"That's a lie, Jack. With a quick phone call I can immediately confiscate your computer. Even if you've erased the hard drive, our lab in Cincinnati can retrieve any data that was on it."

I watched Jack change from a confident young adult to a fumbling, tearful boy, caught in his lie.

"This isn't fair," he babbled, "I didn't spend any of the bills, I just made them. I only wanted to make some quick money." He then proceeded to give Kent the information he needed.

As Jack left, shaken, he turned to me. "I'm sorry, Mr. Pike. I don't know why I thought I could get away with lying. I was so afraid of what my mother would do if she found out."

Ted was a ninth grader, a soccer and basketball player, an average, but hard-working student. His unruly, curly dark hair matched a playful, adventuresome personality. Kent already knew that Ted had spent a number of bills at restaurants and ear X-tacy, a local music store, and had sold several to Sam and George.

Tim arrived with Ted, nervous, his hands trembling. I knew from his parents that he had been arrested last summer for shoplifting a CD.

"What's going on, Mr. Pike?"

"We'll talk about it in a minute, Ted."

Years later I saw Ted at an alumni gathering and asked him about the counterfeiting incident. He had graduated from college and was living at a residential program in Maine for at-risk teenagers, training to become a counselor.

"Oh, that was one of those textbook pieces where teenagers decide not to think about what they're doing and just do it. We were not seeing the big picture, not using our heads, just seeing fake money we can spend. But when you screw up, you might as well be honest. You've already dug the hole and you don't need to go any further."

Ted, having been warned by Dave, had already decided to cooperate and confirmed that he had bought bills from Jack and spent them, that Jack had printed them, and Dave helped sell them.

As a chastened Ted was leaving, I took him aside. "When you go home, tell your parents what happened, all of it, so they hear it first from you. Yes, they'll be hard on you, but you and I both know they will be fair."

Dave and Jack had also tipped off the other boys that it was useless to deny their involvement and the rest of the interviews went smoothly. By the end of his visit, Kent, having lots of experience doing interrogations, seemed as fresh as when he started six hours earlier. Tim and I were exhausted.

Kent was a skilled interrogator—patient, tenacious, firm, even kind. He confirmed whom he suspected made the bills and learned how the other boys obtained bills, where they spent them, and whether they still had any fake twenties in their possession. Having investigated the case for two months, Kent already had most of the answers, an impressive piece of detective work.

"I know this was tough for the two of you, but it went well and I really appreciate your help. I'll go over my notes to make sure I have all the information I need to wrap up the case." He said that he would call us the next day to see how the school wanted to handle the students reimbursing the businesses and that by Monday would have a definitive list of the businesses, their addresses, and how much they were owed.

After Kent left, Tim and I sat in my office and talked for a while. As a teacher, Tim had a lively, interactive lecturing style and knew more about twentieth-century United States history than many college professors. He also knew more about Elvis than most avid Presley fans. As Dean of Students, Tim was unflappable—able to deal decisively and fairly with the most problematic of students.

"You know," he said, "I was disappointed, but not surprised. What concerns me most was their not realizing the serious consequences of what they did."

"You're right. I doubt if any of them would steal twenty dollars, but they seemed clueless that making and spending twenty-dollar bills was far more serious. Thinking it's cool to make passable counterfeit bills on a computer is one thing, but using them is something else." I went on to say that I was particularly angry with Jack and Dave, who thought they were being clever to let the younger kids do the spending. How could they not realize that they would be just as guilty as the spenders?

Tim left for a quick-recall team practice and we agreed to meet the next morning to discuss consequences.

As I continued thinking about the boys, the involvement of Jack and Jim, the sixth boy, especially troubled me. Both were scholarship students from low-income families and part of their motivation was to have money to buy the things their more affluent classmates could buy.

I was curious that all of the students had ended up in tears. Were they fearful of being punished by the school and their parents? Embarrassed by what they had done and being caught so easily? Was it remorse at jeopardizing a school they cared about? When I talked years later with Ted at the alumni gathering, he remembered the worst part of the incident being the shame he felt when classmates told him how dumb he was.

My goal now was to hold the students accountable in just the right way so they learned from their mistakes, without irreparable damage to their futures. I also had to consider legal issues. The words I used when publicly naming students and describing their actions could bring slander suits. If I imposed inappropriate penalties, I could be sued for malpractice.

By the next day, I had to decide what to tell the student body and staff and what punishment to give the boys, to write a letter to parents and the Board of Directors, and to have a response ready if a reporter called me. In any school, rumors start flying immediately when something this unusual and exciting occurs. Over the years I had learned that the best way to deal with rumors is to tell students, staff, and parents as quickly as possible, carefully and directly, the facts—those that could be disclosed—knowing that when I do, the incident may become public. Talk about risk-taking!

The next day, I addressed the counterfeiting incident at Morning Meeting in the Commons Room. Students and staff sat casually on benches, in chairs at tables, and on the carpeted floor. The smells of coffee, EggMcMuffins, and Krispy Kreme donuts wafted through the air. The room buzzed with conversation. In a school this small, the absence of the six boys was obvious. Their friends knew why they weren't there and had told other students. I said, "Quiet please, quiet" in my usual voice—loud, emphatic, a combination of request and command. We had the customary minute of silence that begins the meeting. I knew that students expected me to say something about the incident, as that was my practice. I had everyone's attention.

"Yesterday, Tim Marshall and I spent an unpleasant day watching a Secret Service agent interrogate six of your classmates. Mr. Burnell, the agent, is in charge of a federal investigation of counterfeiting activity by Dave Brooks, Jack Stewart, George McClellan, Mike Larson, Jim Arongo, and Ted Wortham. They are charged with a federal offense, a felony, one for which minors can be prosecuted. These students cheated local businesses by printing and spending $800 worth of counterfeit twenty-dollar bills. They are fortunate that the government has decided not to prosecute as long as any unspent counterfeit bills are returned and businesses compensated for their losses.

What these students did was not only illegal and dishonest, but has damaged the reputation of the St. Francis community. Twenty-five businesses, many of them frequented by you and your classmates, now know that some St. Francis High School students are thieves. All six students have been suspended.

I need everyone to keep conversations about the incident within the school community and to support the students involved in accepting the consequences of their actions.

If you have any questions or concerns about what happened, talk to me or Tim Marshall.

Consider this incident a cautionary tale about computers, which give ready access to information through impersonal electronic media and make it easy to manipulate images and data. While marvelous tools, these features can make it easy to forget what is honest, what is right."

Later that morning, Tim, Janey, and I met in my office to decide the consequences the school would give the six students in addition to those imposed by Special Agent Burnell. Tim and I tended to be theoretical; Janey, as usual, was concrete and practical, no-nonsense in every way; she kept us on task.

When dealing with major offenses, such as cheating, stealing, cutting school, and use of alcohol and other drugs, the criteria we used were simple: what consequences best met the need of individual students to learn from their mistakes and the need of the school community to hold its members responsible for their actions? And, we considered precedent.

"According to Kent Burnell," I began, "all six boys broke the law. Their actions also undermined the trust among students and adults at St. Francis. So shouldn't they get equal punishment?"

Tim argued that, while the law may view the boys equally guilty, from the school's point of view he wasn't sure. Jack, who made the bills and Dave, the main distributor, didn't spend any. Yet their actions created the incident. Janey felt that, as older students, Dave and Jack deserved harsher consequences than the three ninth graders.

We agreed to give Jack and Dave greater penalties. They would not be allowed to participate in any remaining extracurricular school activities, except for graduation. This included prom and, in Dave's case, a school-sponsored summer trip to France. Jack was allowed to finish the track season so as not to penalize the team, but had to withdraw from the prestigious six-week Governor's Scholars Program and forfeit a summer study grant from the school.

In addition to being suspended, the six boys were required to pay back the businesses (approximately $120 per student) and to make an apology in writing and in person, accompanied by a parent. They also posted written apologies to the school community and forfeited any awards they were to receive at the upcoming Awards Assembly.

I met with each of the students and their parents; four of the meetings went well. While these parents were upset, they were relieved that their sons were not being prosecuted by the government or expelled from school.

Jack's mother, Karen, a single parent who idolized her only son, was in shock and disbelief. "Oh my God," she moaned, "no, no."

As I went over what Jack had done, Karen alternated between uncontrollable sobbing and yelling at him. He and I finally calmed her down, and, for the balance of the meeting, she just kept apologizing for him.

The most difficult meeting was with Dave's mother and father, who had already expressed their displeasure over the phone. Dr. and Mrs. Brooks were irate. They believed that the punishment given their son was excessively severe. They came into my office tense and angry.

"What you have done to Dave is outrageous and totally unacceptable. He was the least guilty, yet you threw the book at him."

"He's being persecuted," Mrs. Brooks added. "He's the only senior and it's not fair that he can't go to the prom. And no other student lost the Paris trip. It was his graduation present."

"I understand Dave being upset about the trip," I patiently responded, "but, had any of the others been on the trip, they also would not be going. Dave was the only senior involved. He was the primary distributor to the younger students. Dave is the only one of the six who is 18. He's lucky not to be in jail with a felony on his record."

"I take that to mean you will not consider changing your mind?"

"Yes. His consequences are fair to him and to the school."

Dr. and Mrs. Brooks left more upset than when they had arrived. Their strong feelings of injustice troubled me, as I pride myself on being a fair person. Their reaction was as much a surprise to me as their son's involvement. They never realized that, had their son been at any other school, he most likely would have been expelled and would not have graduated. To his credit, Dave himself handled the situation well, as did all the other students, confirming that they viewed the consequences as fair.

That afternoon, I sent a letter to all parents. Not naming the students, I described what the boys had done and the actions of the Secret Service agent. I said that the students involved would be allowed to complete the year, contingent on their compliance with the conditions set by the school and the government.

I received several supportive notes and phone calls, but one parent, whose daughter was a junior, sent a scathingly critical letter. He was incredulous that the school had not dismissed the students. "They need to be taught a lesson. They all should have been expelled immediately." He went on to say that he had never approved of the school's progressive philosophy. If his daughter weren't going into her senior year and didn't love the school so much, he would have withdrawn her.

Adolescents are risk-takers. Inevitably, part of the maturation process is making mistakes. Staying a step ahead of teenage impulsiveness is one of the challenges of working with adolescents. Teenagers typically live and act in the present moment. These boys were shortsighted, impulsive teenagers, not criminals. They needed significant, but fair consequences and a second chance by adults whom they knew and respected.

The incident didn't make the news. I never knew if the government brought pressure to keep things quiet. It's also possible that friends with the news media decided it wasn't really newsworthy. Maybe I was just lucky. Many risk-takers are.

# 20

## SENIOR PROJECTS

As I walked down the hall from my office, I heard loud, animated voices. Entering the room I was surprised to see virtually all of the senior parents. Uh oh, I thought. They had come in response to a letter from two veteran faculty members, Gail Stone, Senior Project Coordinator, and Dean of Faculty Stanley Conte. Gail and Stan were responsible for implementing Senior Projects, a new graduation requirement. I came to the meeting to introduce the two teachers and to hear for myself parental reactions and concerns about the new program. I knew that some of the seniors had been complaining and that Gail had received phone calls from several parents.

I hoped Stan and Gail were well prepared. Like other teachers, they spent their working days with students, not adults. They were used to dealing with parents individually at parent-teacher conferences, whereas I had lots of practice with groups. I also remember thinking that the letter had a condescending tone, characteristic of Stan, a superb history teacher, intellectually gifted, patient with students, but with little tolerance for uninformed adults.

I welcomed the parents, commented that I hoped the packet sent to them a month ago had been informative, and introduced Gail and Stan. Gail spoke first and explained that the students had been introduced to the Senior Project at the beginning of their junior year. By January over half of them had submitted a topic and chosen an advisor. She reported that virtually all of the then-juniors had handed in proposals by the deadline of April 15, which were approved before the end of the school year. Some students had already started work and the presentation of the first completed project, Summer Esterbrook's, was scheduled in two weeks.

That somebody else's kid was already finishing her project was not what most of the parents wanted to hear. They spoke out in frustration and worry.

"This senior project is just one more thing added to a stressful year of college admissions, hard AP courses, athletics, and social life."

"They don't need a new obstacle to graduation."

"There's just not enough time."

"We had a contract when we came in the ninth grade. It's not fair to add a new requirement in midstream."

"My daughter is totally freaked out about the project. She's afraid she won't graduate."

The outpouring of concern overwhelmed Gail and Stan. They tried to calm things down by describing in unnecessary detail the extra time given to seniors to work on their projects. Unfortunately, some of their information was incorrect and confusing. Also problematic was Stan's statement implying that, while broader in scope, the Senior Project would require no more time than the former research paper, which he described erroneously as a thirty-five-page paper. Everyone left the meeting frustrated.

Two days later I received a three-page single-spaced typed letter from a senior mother, a physician.

... This new change from a senior paper to a senior project is a major change and shrouded in confusion.... What has actually been communicated to the students varies significantly to what you were telling the parents at that meeting.

... The other parents and I came to the meeting to discuss, clarify and speak to you concerning the well being of our children. I feel that you were incredibly arrogant in patronizing us as 'nervous nellies,' overly stressed out parents. We came to you to express our very legitimate concerns and were mostly dismissed in that 'father knows best' attitude.... It is only arrogance for you to believe that you really know what goes on in our child's daily life. We were there in an attempt to help educate you—if you chose to listen.

... Please understand that I don't like being misled or patronized. There is no need to reply in writing to this letter, your future actions will suffice.

As I read the letter, I recognized my own culpability for not planning the meeting more carefully. I should have been ready for the extent of parental concern and predicted Stan's and Gail's lack of skill and experience to defuse it. I could have started the meeting with a reminder of St. Francis High School's focus on developing independent thought and action, one of the reasons they chose the school.

Schools and parents have distinct functions in preparing youth to function successfully without us on a college campus, in a job, in the adult world. Parents referring to the seniors as "our children" was a clear indication that we have different roles. I never think of high school students as children. They are teenagers, adolescents, adults-in-training.

High school is the transition between home and being out in the world as a young adult. St. Francis High School's mission, its design, is to provide a series of increasingly difficult tasks concurrently with giving students the knowledge and skills to accomplish them. The Senior Project was envisioned and implemented as an "exit project," a final challenge, a final exam of readiness for independence.

The school-parent partnership has an inherent tension. The school is pulling adolescents away from parents toward autonomy. At the same time, parents ideally provide a secure foundation, which helps the school to do its job, but overprotectiveness can restrict teenagers' need for independence. To create a productive balance between the two roles, both parties need to be able to talk and listen to each other.

A week later I sent a letter to all senior parents correcting and clarifying information given to them at the meeting. I concluded with a short version of what I should have said as an opening statement at the meeting.

We believe that Senior Projects are a natural and important component of the special education that St. Francis High School gives its students to prepare them personally and academically for college expectations. We see Senior Projects as an enhancement to graduation, not an obstacle to it. We are committed to providing whatever direction and assistance is needed to ensure their satisfactory completion. In addition to helping students, we are available throughout the process to answer your questions and listen to your concerns.

As the 1999-2000 school year progressed, there were no more letters or phone calls of complaints about the projects. Students accepted the reality of the new graduation requirement, some with excitement, others with begrudging acceptance.

At the end of year staff meeting, Gail Stone announced that all seniors had successfully completed their Senior Projects, a third of them earning honors. The consensus of the staff was that Senior Projects were an important addition to the St. Francis curriculum and their inclusion as a requirement for graduation was warranted. No further parent/student uprisings occurred, but the memory of that meeting in September 1999 reminded me of an often-observed trait of adolescence. Teenagers readily agitate for change, want change, but when it arrives they often respond with discomfort and resistance. "It's not fair, Mr. Pike. Last year's class didn't have to do projects."

Maintaining appropriate boundaries is an inherent challenge in being a teacher or parent of a teenager. We can so easily project, insert, our own agendas. In guiding these young adults, keeping an objective perspective is often difficult. Adults are supposed to have learned the lessons in maturity their students are still grappling with. But for our teachers to connect with students individually, they also need to have kept in touch with the spontaneous and impulsive reactions of adolescence. This balance can be difficult to maintain. In the spring of 2002, Mark Cooke's Senior Project prompted a classic example of inappropriate adult behavior. Mark's project was to write a one-act play. Jessie Goodwin, his faculty advisor, was director of St. Francis' drama program and known for choosing contemporary plays which her teenage thespians loved performing. Plays like William Inge's *Bus Stop*, Alfred Uhry's *The Last Night of Ballyhoo*, and Christopher Durang's *The Marriage of Bette and Boo* are not usual fare for high school actors or audiences in terms of subject or language.

Mark enjoyed playing outrageous characters and his original play *Jar Jar Binx* gave ample opportunity to display his talents as writer and actor. Bright, self-centered, Mark also had a large ego and sense of entitlement. *Jar Jar Binx* was performed as part of the annual March showcase of plays written and directed by students. Jessie helped him select three evaluators who would grade his project, which, like all Senior Projects, was required to have three components: research, writing, and presentation. The evaluators were St. Francis teachers, all with interest and experience in drama. While they attended performances of *Jar Jar Binx*, the presentation component of his project, Mark neglected to provide them with any written information, including the required research bibliography. Although Mark had received written and verbal reminders from Gail Stone on several occasions during the previous year and a half, he persisted in believing that the actual performance of his play constituted the Senior Project, rather than being one of three components.

After seeing the play, the three evaluators requested material on the research and written components. Mark placed drafts, revisions, the performed script, and a few research notes in a binder, which was circulated among the evaluators. Jessie, his advisor, suggested that she and Mark meet with the three graders to discuss the play. They met during a lunch period and the graders led Mark through a series of questions to which his responses were brief and superficial. John felt that Mark hadn't given the process of playwriting much thought and Sally questioned the dramatic necessity of what she viewed as excessively vulgar, crude language in the play.

The three evaluators individually filled out the evaluation forms and submitted them to Gail. Senior Project rules call for the three components to be scored separately on a scale of 1 to 5 and then added together to get an overall grade, with 9 being passing and 12 or higher earning honors. Evaluators then meet to discuss their ratings and, if possible, reach a consensus for each component.

George Cooper began the evaluator's meeting by telling John Miller and Sally Thompson that the play was outstanding and Mark deserved honors for his Senior Project. George was incredulous that Sally and John did not agree with him. While they agreed on a 3 for the weak research, they could not reach consensus on scores for the other two components. Sally had to leave to go to class before she had a chance to say anything. After she left, George cursed her, and then added "That's just like her, if she can't have it her way, she walks out." His vehement reaction appalled John. When I later talked with Sally, she hadn't heard George make the comment and was shocked when John told her about it. She had left the meeting in frustration because George talked right past her to John and when she tried to speak he interrupted her.

After Sally left, John and George continued to argue about scoring the presentation component. George was adamant that only the actual performance of the play counted. John felt equally strongly that Mark should provide reflection on the two performances. The meeting ended with George insisting that John write out specific details of his concerns. Later that day, John talked with Dean of Faculty Stan Conte about George's belligerent behavior and unwaveringly narrow interpretation of the presentation component. Stan told John that consensus was not necessary. If a project's evaluators cannot come to an agreement on ratings for a component, the score is based on the average of the three individual scores.

When John arrived at school the next day, coordinator Gail informed him that George had called her the previous night questioning Sally and John's grades of Mark's project. She wanted to meet with all three evaluators. But John and Sally refused to meet again with George, so Gail, Stan, John, and Sally met. John and Sally gave intelligent, thoughtful responses to George's concerns. All four felt that he had gone overboard in his championing of Mark.

Since consensus could not be reached on the written and presentation components, the scores were averaged, which gave Mark an 11.5 grade, missing honors by half a point. Gail filled out a Senior Project grade report and posted it on the student message board for Mark. Later that day she was in her office talking with Stan when Mark came in cursing loudly about his grade. She informed him that if he wasn't satisfied with the evaluation process he should submit an appeal as allowed under Senior Project rules.

The following day George stopped Gail in the hallway with Mark's sheet in his hand.

"What the hell is going on?"

"George, please, let's go somewhere where students aren't around."

They went into George's room and he started yelling at her.

"Why did you give the report to Mark when I hadn't had a chance to get Sally and John to change their grades?"

"George, cool down. Stan and I met with Sally and John. Your unwillingness to consider other ratings than your own from equally well-educated and knowledgeable colleagues together with the uncivil tone of your disagreement made it impossible to reach a consensus on the ratings. Stan and I followed the Senior Project rules and averaged the written and performance component scores."

"How the hell could you have the meeting without me?"

Gail lost her temper and yelled back at him.

"Why would they want to meet with you when you yell and curse at them?"

Startled, George settled down and talked reasonably about his concerns.

That afternoon George took John aside and apologized for his behavior. But he still insisted that Mark deserved honors for his project, especially after all the effort and time he spent and how much he had learned from doing his play.

Later that day I received a phone call from Mark's father, Ron Carter, a prominent litigator. He was upset by Mark's not receiving honors and by what he perceived as serious problems with the evaluation process. We set a time to meet that afternoon.

Mark's father came in angry, convinced that his son had been wronged and determined to have his grade changed to honors. He was especially concerned that Sally Thompson was biased in her comments, in particular her objections to the crude language. I listened to his allegations and then went through the Senior Project process, starting with Mark and his parents receiving separately, a year and a half earlier in November 2000, detailed information about the goals, expectations, and assessment of the Senior Project. I went step by step through Mark's failure to comply with any deadlines or requested submissions other than the performance of the play and then, when asked, eventually providing a binder containing inadequate work.

"Mr. Carter, Mark's mistaken assumption that the live performance of the play constituted his Senior Project and neglecting the other two components was what kept him from earning honors."

"Mr. Pike, I really disagree. What kept Mark from honors were Sally Thompson's biases and John Miller's insistence that the presentation component include more than the actual performance."

"Mr. Carter, Ms. Thompson is quite knowledgeable about drama and, while she found the language in Mark's play personally offensive, she judged his play on its own merits as clearly evidenced in her written report. Mr. Cooper's unwillingness to consider other ratings than his own from well-qualified colleagues made it impossible to reach a consensus." I added that since Mark was not satisfied with his project grade, he was asked to submit a written appeal, an option for any senior dissatisfied with their evaluation.

Mark brought his appeal the next day to Gail and Stan and apologized for his behavior the day before. His appeal was denied and he and his parents informed. Mr. Carter sent me an angry letter protesting the unfairness of the denial and claimed that Ms. Stone did not undertake an independent review of the decisions made by the individual graders. I wrote back that Dean of Faculty Stan Conte and Ms. Stone had met independently with each grader to obtain their responses to Mark's appeal. Based on the assessment criteria, both Ms. Thomas and Mr. Burns had valid reasons for not giving Mark the higher grades needed to achieve honors.

No one denied the effort Mark had put into the play and all agreed that it was one of the best plays of the evening. But nowhere did the assessment criteria state that "amount of time, effort, and money" spent by the presenter was a criterion. Neither a poorly informed parent nor overzealous faculty advisor should be able to unduly influence the outcome of a carefully designed and implemented exit project requirement such as St. Francis' Senior Projects.

A decade later, seniors still grumble and complain. Some Senior Projects are brilliant and others at first glance mundane, but successful within the limitations of its creator or the inappropriate intervention of parents. Books are published, plays authored and produced, cars rebuilt, landscapes rejuvenated, and dances choreographed and performed. For each senior, the project represents reaching a goal, which they, independently, set for themselves. For each teacher, it's a test of their ability to combine rigor with flexibility and open-mindedness, and to honor the process whether or not they approve of the outcome.

# 21

## THE SACRED

Pluralism is the complex and unavoidable encounter, difficult as it may be, with the multiple religions and cultures that are the very stuff of our world… Unless all of us can encounter one another's religious visions and cultural forms and understand them through dialogue, both critically and self-critically, we cannot begin to live with maturity and integrity in the world house.

Diana Eck, *Encountering God*

At a parents dinner early in the school year, Robert Gupta, parent of a tenth grader, came up to me. He told me that he and his wife were pleased with their daughter's education at St. Francis High School. He went on to say that they were surprised and amused that Mina had learned more about Hinduism at St. Francis than she learned at their Temple. While originally affiliated with the Episcopal Diocese of Kentucky, St. Francis is an independent school and enrolls students from diverse faith traditions with more Catholics and Jews than Episcopalians. The student body and faculty have always represented a diversity of faiths. The school's intent is not to advocate any single belief system, but to encourage study, questioning, dialogue, and the witnessing of one's own values in words and actions. A teenager's personal journey to maturity and their preparation for college are informed and strengthened by the academic study of the world's faith traditions. Since 1995, all ninth- and tenth-grade students take a unique two-year course, World Civilizations and Cultures. Students are engaged in what they study because the questions raised are of keen interest to adolescents: Who am I? Where do I come from? What is real? How do I know what is right? Why do people suffer? Why is there evil in the world?

Many members of established faith traditions find religious pluralism uncomfortable. While students usually understand that the academic study of different religions is just as necessary to their education as studying different forms of government, occasionally some parents do not. One mother, the wife of a Protestant minister and an active member of the school's Education Committee, who had a graduate degree in Christian Ethics, was critical of the world history courses. We had ongoing conversations about the appropriateness of these classes for her teenage daughter.

"Tom, I'm disturbed by what Cathy is being required to read and discuss in her history class. Mr. Collins is deconstructing my daughter's faith. She's too young to be asking these kinds of questions."

She was referring to texts such as *The Ramayana*, the *Bhagavad-Gita, Conference of the Birds*, the poetry of Kabir and Mirabai, selections from the Chinese T'ang poets, as well as several prophetic books from the Hebrew Bible and one of the gospel narratives, all read in conjunction with the study of the history of their respective cultures.

I responded, a bit too quickly. "Susan, I think that you're underestimating your daughter's intellectual ability and maturity. We parents tend not to want our children to grow up, especially when they reach adolescence."

"That really offends me. My concern is based on several years spent examining faith development, especially among children and youth. Fowler is very clear about fifteen- and sixteen-year-old adolescents not being ready for serious exposure to other religious traditions."

I apologized for not being very tactful. "I know you have your daughter's best interests at heart and having her appropriately challenged is one of the reasons you and David enrolled her at St. Francis. I'm familiar with Fowler's stages of faith development and, frankly, I find his approach parochial, simplistic, and based on minimal experience with adolescents. Surely you have considered the possibility that Cathy may eventually decide not to be a Lutheran, maybe not even a practicing Christian?"

Susan reminded me that she was a devout Christian. "I can intellectually accept other people choosing different paths, perhaps even my children when they are adults. I know that being a Lutheran is right for me and I want that certainty for Cathy, especially during the turmoil of adolescence."

"Susan, trust your daughter to become a discerning seeker, intellectually and spiritually. That's the school's goal for all of its students and the reason it was founded. And it is important for Cathy to begin her independent journey in high school, while she still has your example and support."

She could not leave it at that. "I guess that's helpful, Tom. But I think you're a bit hard on Fowler. I need to reread him and we'll have another conversation."

While we had several subsequent talks, eventually we amicably agreed to disagree, and our philosophical differences became irrelevant as Cathy blossomed into an independent young woman. She became a successful student, caring friend, and a captain of both volleyball and basketball teams. I don't know what happened to her Lutheran faith; it had ceased to be a question between us.

Susan Reigler, who taught biology and chemistry, was a devout Darwinian and an agnostic. No student left her class without knowing the difference between a scientific principle, established and revised by verifiable evidence, and a faith belief, not provable by the rules of science. Over the years, she had a handful of conservative Christian students and, while she respected their faith, for her, evolution was a basic law of science. One year, her classes took on a major project to create and illustrate in the school's rear stairwell a timeline of life on planet Earth, starting with the Big Bang at the basement level of the school. Anyone walking up to the third floor traversed four flights of stairs and 4.5 billion years of Earth's existence, depicted by colorful murals of various forms of life present over the millennia. That human history was represented by the last inch of the timeline was a humbling revelation.

When I gave Susan permission to create the illustrated timeline, I never thought about its potential impact on some of the Christians at St. Francis, whose faith required a different timeline and denied the theory of evolution. Every February 12, Susan stood up in Morning Meeting and announced Charles Darwin's birthday. One year, I happened to notice Nancy Gardner's face set in an expression of resignation during Susan's announcement. Nancy, a junior, was a top student, a member of the School Committee, and a talented soccer player, one of a few girls who held their own on a boys team before the advent of girls soccer teams. She and her parents were religiously conservative. I realized that the mural and its visual endorsement of evolution might be offensive to Nancy as she went up and down the stairs every day.

Later that day I saw her sitting against the wall in the main hallway, relaxing during a free period. I knew her fairly well because her father had taught at St. Francis School when I worked there.

I sat down next to her. "I thought about you this morning during Ms. Reigler's announcement of Darwin's birthday. I know your faith does not accept Darwinism and I wondered how you feel every day as you go up and down the rear stairwell seeing the mural depicting evolution."

"I appreciate your concern, Mr. Pike, but it's no big deal. I simply don't see it."

"What did you do last year in biology class when you were required to learn the theory of evolution?"

"I learned it. It's part of the science I need to know to take college courses. I've learned to separate science from my religious beliefs. It's just a part of the game we learn to play. And Ms. Reigler respects my beliefs as I respect hers."

A couple of years later, after considering a number of both public and private high schools, a conservative Southern Indiana couple, Thad and Helen Poole, enrolled their only child Janice. They were convinced after their visit to the school that their daughter would receive the best available preparation for college at St. Francis and that her keen intelligence and religious beliefs would be respected. Janice was a gifted student, National Merit Finalist, and, while reserved, an active participant in school life, including playing four years of interscholastic volleyball.

I was puzzled that such an intellectually gifted student as Janice was a Christian fundamentalist. I was also concerned when she chose to enroll at a small, conservative sectarian college located on a rural Kentucky campus when she could have attended a prestigious, highly selective university farther afield.

Occasionally at Morning Meetings I made brief comments about a current issue or event. One day, early in November, I spoke about celebrating All Saints' Day at my church, the Episcopal cathedral, two blocks from the school. I suggested that saints are individuals inspired by their belief in a divine reality to do special things for God's creation and that such people are part of all religious traditions. I mentioned Mahatma Gandhi, Yitzhak Rabin, Martin Luther King, Jr, and Aung San Suu Ky as striking examples, not necessarily of personal goodness, but of profound faithfulness, who through personal action and risk irrevocably set their nations on new paths towards social justice. Unfortunately, Suu Ky no longer has her former convictions.

After the meeting, virtually everyone left for their first-period class and I noticed Janice sitting quietly in a corner of the Commons Room. I went over and asked if we could talk for a couple of minutes.

"Sure, Mr. Pike. I've got a free period and I'm already prepared for my classes."

"I know that you and your family are people with a strong Christian faith. You've heard me talk before about religious pluralism. The Christian writer C. S. Lewis used the metaphor of mail to describe pluralism. He believed that God had connected powerfully with him through the Christian story and rituals. But this was his mail, mail addressed just to him. Only God could know what mail non-Christians received. Lewis was certain that he received mail from God. But he knew that God could well be sending different, but equally valuable life-changing messages to others. I think that Lewis would have been comfortable this morning when I honored individuals of other faiths as being as divinely inspired as Christian saints. I'm curious to know how my comments sounded to you."

Janice thought for a few minutes. "Lewis' metaphor is interesting and it may work for you and him, but it doesn't work for me. I'm not offended by the idea that non-Christians might receive equally valuable messages from God; I just don't believe they do. I think the problem is that your and Lewis' personal beliefs and your acceptance of religious pluralism are primarily rational constructs. You two men are perennial intellectual seekers. I don't need to keep seeking. My Christian faith is as much a part of me as my eyes and hands. My being saved by Jesus' sacrifice creates an inseparable bond between us." I had perhaps never been so gently put in my place.

While I've never lost sight of the essential Quaker belief that each of us has the divine, the sacred, within us, what that means varies enormously from person to person. I realized that Janice, too, was an adolescent exception and a risk-taker. Her principled refusal simply to accept pluralism's challenge was in its own way as much a rejection of consensus values as Frank Cayce's Fools Friday or the senior prank to end all senior pranks had been. It was not likely a version that Frank or I would have accepted in the early 1970s. But it is a vision that St. Francis High School and I had learned to cultivate, in order that, in Diana Eck's words, our students might, "through dialogue, both critically and self-critically, ... begin to live with maturity and integrity in the world house."

## ABOUT THE AUTHOR

Tom Pike was raised in Louisville, where he graduated from Eastern High School. He studied engineering and philosophy at Stanford University and as a graduate student at Princeton, trained as a teacher and educator, and returned in 1967 as Assistant Headmaster of St. Francis School. In 1977, he became founding Headmaster of St. Francis High School. He retired in 2003 and continues to reside in Louisville.